Praise for
Sun Stand Still

"Pastor Steven Furtick is not normal. The incredible move of God at Elevation Church is not normal. Unfortunately, audacious faith is also not normal. I don't know anyone better positioned to challenge you to rise above mundane living and embrace faith-filled audacity than Steven Furtick. *Sun Stand Still* is a call for us to live with such audacious faith that people like Pastor Steven and churches like Elevation become the norm rather than the exception."

> —CRAIG GROESCHEL, senior pastor, LifeChurch.tv;
> author of *Chazown* and *The Christian Atheist*

"Steven Furtick is one of the freshest and most challenging voices in the church today. In *Sun Stand Still*, he calls all of us to stop merely believing God can do the impossible and instead start expecting him to. This is a must-read for every Christian."

> —JOHNNY HUNT, senior pastor, First Baptist Church,
> Woodstock, Georgia; former president of the
> Southern Baptist Convention; author of *Building
> Your Leadership Resume*

"This book is like a ticking time bomb. It will blow up your small dreams and leave an audacious faith in its place."

> —MARK BATTERSON, lead pastor, National Community
> Church; author of *Primal* and *In a Pit with a Lion
> on a Snowy Day*

"This book is not for the person who believes that God is safe and never calls anyone to dream big dreams. Pastor Steven Furtick sheds light on an Old Testament story and then shows in extremely practical ways how the same God who performed unbelievable miracles 'back then' can do it today—he's just looking for people crazy enough to believe he has not changed."

—PERRY NOBLE, senior pastor, NewSpring Church;
blogger on leadership, vision, and creativity

"In *Sun Stand Still*, my friend Steven Furtick challenges all of us—from the missionary in the third world to the family in the suburbs—to believe God for the impossible and begin living a life of faith beyond the ordinary."

—ANDY STANLEY, senior pastor, North Point
Community Church; author of *How Good
Is Good Enough?* and *The Principle of the Path*

"For too long Christians have embraced a miniscule vision of faith that is satisfied with merely marveling at the miracles we see in the Bible. In *Sun Stand Still*, Steven Furtick reminds us that the God who accomplished the impossible through the great heroes of faith still desires to do the same through us today."

—JENTEZEN FRANKLIN, senior pastor, Free Chapel;
New York Times best-selling author of *Fasting:
Opening the Door to a Deeper, More Intimate,
More Powerful Relationship with God*

"It can be so easy for us to limit God—not in what he can do or who he is but in what we expect of him. Too often we become complacent with merely hoping for God to act, but rarely do we follow through on the belief that he will. In *Sun Stand Still*, my friend Steven Furtick pushes each of us beyond our comfort zone of earthly hope and into the realm of supernatural expectation. This book will show you that your hopes and expectations are truly just the beginning of what God can do."

—ED YOUNG, senior pastor, Fellowship Church;
author of *Outrageous, Contagious Joy*

"In *Sun Stand Still,* Steven Furtick casts a bold vision for what faith was always designed to look like. My friend Steven's combination of passion and practicality will both move you to want to live at a higher level of faith and equip you to get there."

> —ISRAEL HOUGHTON, Grammy Award–winning recording
> artist; worship leader, Lakewood Church

"*Sun Stand Still* invokes the omnipotent power of God by challenging the reader to embrace God's will for our lives by strengthening our faith through prayer. This book is enthralling and moves you to believe in the impossible as you learn to live a life of boldness for the kingdom of God."

> —BISHOP EDDIE LONG, pastor, New Birth Missionary
> Baptist Church; author of *60 Seconds to Greatness*
> and *What a Man Wants, What a Woman Needs*

"Steven Furtick is a catalyst. And *Sun Stand Still* is a must-read. This book will stir you, shake you, and ultimately inspire you. It's a wake-up call for our generation to be audacious, to not settle for the ordinary, and to ask God for the impossible."

> —BRAD LOMENICK, director of Catalyst

"*Sun Stand Still* is a declaration of audacity that will shake you up and propel your faith forward. Steven Furtick is a fresh voice that reads like a cross between Billy Sunday and T. D. Jakes—and that's saying something!"

> —TIM SANDERS, business speaker and consultant;
> author of *Love Is the Killer App*

SUN STAND STILL

WHAT HAPPENS WHEN YOU DARE
TO ASK GOD FOR THE IMPOSSIBLE

STEVEN FURTICK

MULTNOMAH
BOOKS

SUN STAND STILL
PUBLISHED BY MULTNOMAH BOOKS
12265 Oracle Boulevard, Suite 200
Colorado Springs, Colorado 80921

Scripture quotations are taken from the Holy Bible, New International Version®. NIV®. Copyright ©
1973, 1978, 1984 by Biblica Inc.™ Used by permission of Zondervan. All rights reserved worldwide.
www.zondervan.com.

Italics in Scripture quotations reflect the author's added emphasis.

Details in some anecdotes and stories have been changed to protect the identities of the persons involved.

ISBN 978-1-60142-322-1
ISBN 978-1-60142-323-8 (electronic)

Copyright © 2010 by Steven Furtick

Published in the United States by WaterBrook Multnomah, an imprint of the Crown Publishing Group,
a division of Random House Inc., New York.

MULTNOMAH and its mountain colophon are registered trademarks of Random House Inc.

Library of Congress Cataloging-in-Publication Data
Furtick, Steven.
    Sun stand still : what happens when you dare to ask God for the impossible / Steven Furtick.
— 1st ed.
        p. cm.
    ISBN 978-1-60142-322-1 — ISBN 978-1-60142-323-8 (electronic)
    1. Prayer—Christianity. 2. Christian life. 3. Faith. 4. Bible. O.T. Joshua X, 12–13—Criticism,
interpretation, etc. I. Title.
    BV220.F87 2010
    248.3'2—dc22
                                      2010021725

Printed in the United States of America
2010

10 9 8 7 6 5 4

SPECIAL SALES
Most WaterBrook Multnomah books are available at special quantity discounts when purchased in bulk
by corporations, organizations, and special-interest groups. Custom imprinting or excerpting can also be
done to fit special needs. For information, please e-mail SpecialMarkets@WaterBrookMultnomah.com
or call 1-800-603-7051.

To all the Elevators who believe. Heart and soul.

Contents

Contents

Contents

This Is How It Feels

I can't lie—it's a pretty cool feeling to have Bono as your opening act. Even if his show was four and a half years before ours.

My friend Eric was the first one to make the connection for me. He brought it up as we drove past the seemingly endless line of people waiting outside the Time Warner Cable Arena in Charlotte, North Carolina. It was Easter Sunday 2010. The people were all hoping to get in the front door for the Elevation Church Easter service. Seeing how the line of people wrapped around the building took my breath away.

Taking in the scene, Eric asked, "Remember when we were standing in that same line when we first moved here? Waiting for the U2 show?"

"Yeah. Kind of. That seems like a lifetime ago."

"Remember what you said to me when The Edge started playing the opening riff of 'City of Blinding Lights'? You were screaming over the music. You looked up toward the nosebleed section and told me that one day our church would fill that arena for a worship service."

"I did, didn't I?" It was all coming back to me.

"You did. You said that. Did you really believe it would happen?"

"Yeah. I did. I really believed."

"Well, it's happening. Right now. Look at all those people. This is crazy."

"Yeah. It is crazy."

But the truth is, "crazy" didn't come close to describing it. This moment at this arena was the most surreal moment of my life. It was a culmination of the most audacious dream I have ever dared to entertain. And the dream was coming true.

See, just four and a half years earlier, I was a twenty-five-year-old kid moving to a new city with a few other like-minded families in tow. We had no connections. Very little strategy. Even less experience. Just a dream to start a church and change the world. And a whole lot of faith.

Now, in about an hour, I'd be stepping onto the stage to preach to well over ten thousand people in the largest venue in our city. This was our church. This was our moment. This was God's answer to our prayers and the reward of our faith.

I was about to preach the gospel from the same spot where I watched one of the biggest rock bands in the world play "Where the Streets Have No Name." I don't know which sensation was stronger—the thousands of memories per second flashing like a strobe light in my brain, reminding me of all the experiences that had led up to this day, or the anticipation of what God would accomplish in the moments ahead when—as it turned out—hundreds of people responded to the invitation to receive Christ and begin a brand-new life, changing our city forever.

This is how it feels to share the stage with Bono.

This is how it feels to believe God for the impossible.

This is how it feels to see the sun stand still...

CHAPTER 1

Welcome to Audacious Faith

Pastor Michael proudly showed me the place where his church was putting in new toilets. I was still adjusting to the smell, trying to pass it off like it didn't faze me. Like I walked down urine-soaked dirt roads every day.

"These toilets would not be very nice by the standards of your country," Michael explained. "I know that. But here in the slums of Kampala, Uganda, so many children are sick because the food they eat is cooked right next to the hole in the ground where they go to the bathroom. So our church is building the nicest toilets we can here...for the children."

I had a hard time concentrating as he went on laying out his plans. Because as soon as he said the word "children," my gaze drifted to a cluster of kids playing some variation of Capture the Flag on the trash heap behind the church. The church was really just a shed. And instead of a flag, the kids appeared to be competing for an orange peel. It was weird how content these kids seemed, playing with just a peel—more content, it appeared to me, than a lot of kids back home seem playing with a Wii. And this garbage heap here on the edge of Pastor Michael's church property looked like the neighborhood hot spot. How, I wondered, would parents of elementary-school kids at my church react if they were asked to drop their children off at a playground like this one?

Pastor Michael's church members obviously weren't worried about it. They had been under the shed worshiping loudly for about an hour, and I realized they thought nothing of the fact that there was a small goat eating breakfast on top of the trash heap right next to where their kids were tossing around the orange peel. A scrawny, hungry, scary-looking goat.

Michael must have noticed that I was taking in the scene. "This is a Muslim hill," he continued, yanking my attention back to our conversation. "I am used to facing a lot of opposition. A lot of people do not want me here. Especially the witch doctor who tried to destroy our church by threatening our members. But when we prayed for God to make fire fall down from heaven, and his house burned down that same week, he left us alone."

I shot him a questioning look.

"Do not worry," he said, a twinkle in his eye. "He was not home at the time."

For the rest of the tour, I could barely keep up with Pastor Michael. He was moving fast and talking even faster. I felt clumsy and white trying to dodge the mud puddles while he led me down alleys through the slum. This was his village, he said. With every step, he detailed how he wanted to transform it for Christ. A school on this lot. A doctor's office on that lot.

"For the children," he kept saying…

Tonia could act like a total diva if she wanted to. She's pretty, well paid, locally famous, and uber talented. So people in our community are noticeably shocked when they show up to help serve breakfast at a homeless shelter and see Tonia in the kitchen making scrambled eggs.

It happened the other day. She was volunteering with an outreach group from our church when somebody asked me, "Isn't that the lady from the news?"

"Yeah, that's Tonia. She's awesome."

"What's she doing here?"

"She's serving."

"Huh. Wow. That's impressive."

Actually, I would describe the way Tonia does her life as a few notches above impressive. I'd characterize it as *audacious.*

Strictly according to her job title, she is a news anchor—a multiple-award-winning one at that. But *news anchor* doesn't begin to capture the essence of who Tonia is. She's a community service superhero who has designed her life around leveraging her on-camera talent to make an off-camera impact. She's better at it than anyone else I've ever met. Charlotte is filled with teen moms, homeless families, and shut-ins who have been touched by Tonia's passion to serve. And she's relentless about recruiting others to serve with her.

In her latest project, she set out to convince thousands to join her for an initiative called Love Week. She was asking them to commit to giving five thousand hours of service to the city. In a single week. It had never been done before.

I can't say I was surprised when I heard that Love Week added up to more than ten thousand service hours. That's just how Tonia rolls. When she gets a vision, it usually sounds a little out there. People try to explain to her that it's never been done before. And I think she likes it that way. If it's necessary, and it's never been done, she seems to assume that's because God intends for her to do it.

To the untrained eye a pastor standing in the slums of Kampala, Uganda, and a news anchor scrambling eggs in Charlotte, North Carolina, don't have much in common. The challenges they face are as different as the hemispheres where they live. But I see them as twins. They share the same spiritual DNA. They're driven by the same passion. They accomplish ridiculously amazing things for God's glory. Their faith seems to be turbocharged from some source that the average Christian never quite taps into.

It's hard to define exactly what sets Michael and Tonia apart from other people who claim to believe the same things they believe but lead, by contrast, mediocre lives. Most believers I've met actually *do* want to find the source of Michael's and Tonia's high-octane faith—and they want it desperately. They just don't know where to look for it.

Sun Stand Still is all about discovering that kind of faith. I call it *audacious faith*. By the time you finish this book, the same faith that pulses in Michael's and Tonia's everyday life will be pumping through your veins too. You'll understand that God has much more in mind for your existence on this earth than merely surviving. What you consider possible for your life will expand beyond anything you've ever imagined. And the way you approach God and experience him every day will change too. Radically. Suddenly. Irreversibly.

But first, some honest disclosure.

A THEOLOGY OF AUDACITY

This book is not a Snuggie.

The words on these pages will not go down like Ambien.

I'm not writing to calm or coddle you.

With God's help, I intend to incite a riot in your mind. Trip your breakers and turn out the lights in your favorite hiding places of insecurity and fear. Then flip the switch back on so that God's truth can illuminate the divine destiny that may have been lying dormant inside you for years. In short, I'm out to activate your audacious faith. To inspire you to ask God for the impossible. And in the process, to reconnect you with your God-sized purpose and potential.

You could think of this book as a one-volume theology of audacity. You probably don't have one of those yet, but it's essential. In fact, if you ever encounter a theology that doesn't directly connect the greatness of God with your potential to do great things on his behalf, it's not biblical theology. File it under heresy.

I'll take that further: if you're not daring to believe God for the impossible, you're sleeping through some of the best parts of your Christian life.

And further still: if the size of your vision for your life isn't intimidating to you, there's a good chance it's insulting to God.

Audacious faith is the raw material that authentic Christianity is made of. It's the stuff that triggers ordinarily level-headed people like you and me to start living with unusual boldness. When you live this way, your eyes will be opened to see your day-to-day life in vivid color. Your spiritual growth will accelerate at a supernatural pace.

If you're like most Christians, *audacity* is not a word you use to describe your faith. *Audacity,* my dictionary says, makes regular people behave with "boldness or daring, especially with confident disregard for personal comfort [or] conventional thought." And, if you think about it, confident disregard for the status quo is the essence of the gospel. It describes the radical path Christ's life took on earth. It goes to the heart of what it means to live by faith.

Of course, every believer in Jesus has a measure of faith—it's the prerequisite to salvation. But after that, if we're honest, we think of faith primarily in terms of a spiritual thought or a comfortable feeling. We hope it's enough to get us to heaven when we die. But in the meantime, it's barely enough to keep us praying, giving, and going to the eleven o'clock service.

Let me ask you: does the brand of faith you live by produce the kinds of results in your life that you read about in the biblical stories of men and women of faith?

Chances are, not even close.

For most of us, this disparity is hard to live with. The chasm we see between our mundane spiritual experiences and the overcoming faith we read about in the accounts of biblical heroes is downright discouraging. It can create a heavy weight of condemnation and a sense of failure in our hearts. We can begin to feel like maybe our faith isn't the real thing. Some believers I've known have gotten so tired of faking faith that they have just given up altogether.

Posttraumatic Faith Disorder

I'll admit that faith is a sore subject for millions. It's been abused, mishandled, distorted, and ultimately disfigured. Sometimes it seems like there's a custom-tailored faith for everyone:

✳ If the Galatians 2:20 kind of faith—"I have been crucified with Christ and I no longer live, but Christ lives in me. The life I live in the body, I live by *faith* in the Son of God, who loved me and gave himself for me"—is too clunky for you, trade it in. Exchange it for an easier, no-money-down model.

✳ If trusting in the miracle-working power of Jesus is too *out there* for your modern mind, play it safe. Don't ever ask God to provide for you supernaturally. Don't dare to ask for physical healing or anything else that would put God on the spot. Because what if he *doesn't* come through?

A lot of Christians I know stagger through life in a daze. Suffering from posttraumatic faith disorder, they hunker down in the basement, open a can of Beanie Weenees, and wait for the end of the world.

Am I reading your mail? If so, you're probably stuck in spiritual survival mode. You've settled for spiritual mediocrity. You're not trying to be a hypocrite. It's just that so far the faith thing hasn't, well, *worked* for you.

But we can't let abuses and misunderstandings hold us back. God has no Plan B. The Bible throws down the gauntlet in Hebrews 11:6:

Without faith it is impossible to please God.

It doesn't get any plainer than that. Faith isn't just a Get Out of Hell Free card. It's the most vital building block of your relationship with God. And it's the only real foundation worth establishing your life on.

We can't abandon the life-changing promise of full-frontal faith because some have dealt with the topic recklessly and unbiblically. It would be a shame for us to let bad experiences or past disappointments keep us bound, poor, and blind to what God wants to do in our lives.

We've got to find a better way.

THERE IS A HIGHER LEVEL

You're about to discover what happens when you dare to *believe* God for the impossible, *ask* God for the impossible—then *act* in audacious faith for his glory.

You're about to discover that faith is not a drug to sedate you through a life you hate. It's a force to transport you to another realm of reality.

There *is* a better way—a higher calling to fulfillment and significance that God deeply desires for your job, your marriage, your parenting, your finances, and your impact on this world.

That kind of life may be a long way off from where you live and breathe right now. And it may take a little convincing before you believe this kind of life is even an option for you.

Maybe it will help if I introduce you to a man who experienced firsthand what happens when you live with audacity, believing God for the impossible. You're already a lot more like him than you think.

CHAPTER 2

Prayer That Stops the Sun

Enter Joshua, one of the great franchise players of the Old Testament. Most people with a scrap of Bible knowledge or a few days in Vacation Bible School know that Joshua fought the battle of Jericho. But his epic story started long before that.

Born into slavery—the fate of every Jew of his generation—Joshua grew up to experience firsthand Israel's deliverance from Egyptian oppression. On the journey to the Promised Land, he rose to a position of leadership as Moses' assistant. Then, at the very border of the Promised Land, disaster struck. When the people heard that giants and walled cities stood between them and taking possession of their destiny, they panicked. Everyone wanted to turn back.

Everyone, that is, except Joshua and his friend Caleb. Maybe you know the story. Unlike the other spies, Joshua and Caleb returned from scouting out the Promised Land with a message of faith, not fear:

> The land we passed through and explored is exceedingly
> good. If the LORD is pleased with us, he will lead us into that

land, a land flowing with milk and honey, and will give it to us. Only do not rebel against the LORD. And do not be afraid of the people of the land, because we will swallow them up. (Numbers 14:7–9)

But fear won out that day. God's people didn't understand that if you want to experience God's blessings, audacious faith is not optional. Even after all the miracles they'd witnessed in the desert, they still hadn't grasped that what seemed impossible for them to accomplish was exactly what God wanted to accomplish for them.

Forty wasted years followed.

I feel for Joshua. To my mind, forty years of enduring the consequences of other people's bad decision would be enough to derail anybody's faith. Yet Joshua never flinched. He never gave in. He never lost sight of God's promises. And when Moses died, God chose Joshua to be his successor. Big shoes to fill. Most ordinary believers would back down, but Joshua stepped up.

He launched a campaign activated by audacious faith in God's goodness and power. And Joshua changed the world in his generation.

Think about it: Before Joshua took charge, God's people were migrants, living hand to mouth. Afterward, they were settlers— owners of the "exceedingly good" land God had promised.

At this point it would be totally understandable if you're thinking, *I'm not sure I see how a Bible hero's military campaign relates to my life. My most exciting daily battles are navigating stop-and-go traffic at 7:30 a.m. without doing violence to anyone, on the way to a job I'd give anything to quit, and getting my kids to clean their rooms at night without any bloodshed.*

I feel you. But stay with me. The story God has scripted for your life isn't inferior to Joshua's—or anyone else's. There's an exceedingly good land that you're meant to occupy. And as you put yourself in this story, something life changing will begin to happen inside you.

The Audacity to Ask

My favorite exploit in Joshua's life doesn't get nearly enough airtime, if you ask me. From every angle, the story—tucked away in Joshua 10—showcases the kind of audacity we're after. And it all hinges on a preposterous prayer. In fact, when you first hear it, you might even feel like it's insulting or irreverent. But as it turns out, our God isn't intimidated by long-shot prayers.

As the chapter opens, we read that five opposing Amorite armies were planning to attack. Having decided to strike first, Joshua led his entire army toward the Amorites on an all-night march. Sometime during that march, God spoke to Joshua. He told him:

Do not be afraid of them; I have given them into your hand.
Not one of them will be able to withstand you. (verse 8)

At dawn, the Israelites unleashed a surprise attack, and right from the beginning the battle went well. When the enemy lines broke, and the Amorites started to flee into the valley, Joshua's men chased them down. And God got personally involved. "As they fled before Israel," the account reads, "the LORD hurled large hailstones down on them from the sky" (verse 11).

Then, as the sun sank toward the horizon, Joshua faced a

decision. The victory wasn't complete, and once it got dark, the rest of the Amorites would slip away. But Joshua was determined to fight on. Perhaps he realized that if he didn't destroy the enemy now, Israel's conquest of Canaan would grind to a halt. Maybe he knew that anything less than total victory would conceal God's presence and glory. Besides, he remembered God's promise in the night: "Not one of them will be able to withstand you."

Most of us—even really good Christian people—would have called it a day. *I've done all I can do. I've exhausted every option. I've given it all I've got.* But Joshua wasn't most people. He refused to go out like that. That wasn't the way it was supposed to end. This was where his audacious faith began.

Joshua sized up the situation, summoned all his available courage, and delivered one of the most gloriously unorthodox prayers in the entire Bible:

O sun, stand still over Gibeon,
O moon, over the Valley of Aijalon. (verse 12)

Now can you see why I love this story? Joshua had the audacity to ask God to make the sun stop in the sky. To freeze time on behalf of his people.

I know this proposition seems impossible to us. And it doesn't make a bit of sense scientifically. But according to Scripture, God gave Joshua exactly what he ordered. Just when the Amorites were hanging on for the cover of darkness, darkness never came. Just when they thought the curtains were about to drop on their day from hell, God came out for an encore.

The sun stopped in the middle of the sky and delayed going down about a full day. There has never been a day like it before or since…. Surely the LORD was fighting for Israel! (verses 13–14)

The skeptic in me has all kinds of questions: Did God actually stop the earth on its axis? Did he create some kind of substitute sun to extend daylight? In other words, what really went down here?

I don't know the answers to those questions. There are other books written by much smarter people that address the practical implications of this event. But my faith is pretty simple. I choose to believe that the same God who intervened to bring his Son back to life intervened on this day in history to help his people. He chose to answer Joshua's outrageous prayer. He did what only he could do. And he did it in a way that his people would never forget—in a way that we're still marveling at to this day.

Besides, maybe instead of trying to figure out all the technical answers, we should be asking a more relevant question: could it be that God intends for us to have the same kind of audacious faith—the kind of faith that dares to believe God for the impossible—as a normal way of life?

With everything in me, I believe he does. I believe he still desires to make the sun stand still over the life of every believer. If we'll have the audacity to ask.

IN THE MIDDLE OF A MOVE OF GOD

I tried this one time. I'll tell you about it if you'll promise not to laugh.

I started this book by describing to you how breathtaking it was to lead a worship service with over ten thousand people in attendance. But trust me, my journey as a pastor certainly didn't begin that way. It all started with a God-given, gospel-centered, audacious ambition. My wife and I moved to Charlotte with a four-month-old kid, limited funding, no connections, and little experience. In faith, seven other families moved with us. We had been meeting with these families for almost a year, laying the foundation for a church that I had been dreaming about starting since my junior year of high school. I just didn't know where. Or when. Or how. Only why.

We set a goal of reaching over one thousand people in our first year of ministry. Since the average church size in America is fewer than one hundred and twenty, and the first rule of goal setting is attainability, I guess we were overshooting a bit. But we wanted to see God accomplish something so exponentially amazing that it would leave no doubt who deserved the credit. In fact, several times during those months of casting vision, I told our little group, "I want to know what it means to live life and do ministry at the speed of God. I want to see God do so much so fast that the world will have to take note."

So we shamelessly asked God to exceed our wildest dreams and bring unprecedented Kingdom success to our very first year of ministry.

Some people laughed at our approach. I guess in their eyes we might as well have been shouting at the sun, insisting that it stop in its tracks. Their skepticism was understandable. Charlotte is one of the most "overchurched" cities in America—more than eight hundred churches at last count. (Bonus: it's the birthplace of Billy Graham.) Why would Charlotte need *another* church? As a matter of fact, some church-growth experts refer to Charlotte as a church-planting graveyard.

A few of those experts reinforced the intimidation I felt during my first few months. "Welcome to the neighborhood, kid," they'd say. "You might want to consider renting your house instead of buying." One told us that nine out of ten new churches here fail before the three-year mark. "Good luck, though," he said. "If I can do anything to help…"

I spent some long nights nursing regrets. More than once I wished I could take the whole thing back. I had convinced seven families to sell houses, quit jobs, and move to Charlotte. No salaries. No benefits. Just a burning conviction that there has to be more to life than a 401(k), additional square footage, soccer leagues, and church as usual. I really wanted to believe. But honestly, at times I wondered.

If you've ever set out to accomplish a dream that was just too big for you, I know you can relate. Maybe for you it was a business venture, a physical healing, a family reconciliation, a set of values you wanted to pass on to your children against all odds, or a relationship you desperately desired. When you have a dream in your heart, but no earthly idea how to make it happen, keeping your faith intact is a full-time job. But I've discovered that these crises of belief don't have to be the end of faith. They can become the foundation that a stronger faith is built on.

Surely Joshua faced the temptation to stop believing. Surely he must have been overcome by doubt before *and* after his outrageous request that God would reset the solar clock. But we can only speculate, because the Bible only records what mattered to God: Joshua's faith and Joshua's prayer…and what God did next.

He stopped the sun. He accomplished the impossible.

Don't you want a piece of that kind of divine action?

Wouldn't you like to know how it feels to see God accomplish the impossible right in front of your eyes? While I can't relate to the scope of Joshua's challenges or conquests, I am captivated by his faith. However it might come across, I might as well tell you up front that *I intend to live this way.* I'm determined to take ground and win big for the kingdom of God. I'm unapologetic about my mission to change my world for the glory of Jesus. I want to be a Joshua in my generation.

The story of our church is still being told, of course. But here's what I can tell you now. After just four years of ministry, our church has grown to more than six thousand regular attendees. Since our opening day, more than five thousand people have publicly professed faith in Christ. I'll never forget the time we baptized over a thousand adults in a two-week period. And the Easter service I told you about? Over seven hundred people committed their lives to Christ on that single Sunday.

And we're just getting started. Sometimes, when we consider the rate at which God has multiplied this ministry, we feel like we're living in a warp-speed dream world. But the story is real, and our city is shaking. We feel the tremors all around us. We are living in the middle of a move of God.

We've seen previously suicidal teenagers maturing in the things of God, leading their friends to Christ, and showing up at 5:00 a.m. on Sunday to volunteer.

We've seen couples come to our church with the intention of giving God one last try before signing their divorce papers. A few months later, we've seen their marriages restored: families healing, faith growing, new life emerging.

We've seen God multiply meager financial resources like the fish and loaves over and over again.

We've seen people who have been terrified to even talk about their faith in the office lead their same co-workers on a missions trip to a country that is hostile to the gospel.

I guess you could say we have seen the sun stand still.

But this book isn't about us. It's about what God stands ready to do for and through you. I believe our story hints at a God-sized transformation that is available to every follower of Christ.

ACTIVATING AUDACIOUS FAITH

I'm inviting you to be a main character in the story, in the thick of the plot. What God has done among us is so big that there's nobody to blame but him. I want you to be able to say the same about your life. I want you to take the chance on another kind of faith. I want you to live in the middle of a move of God.

There's nothing our world needs more desperately today—in individuals, families, businesses, churches, and communities—than God's saving, supernatural acts. And he's ready to act if we will be bold enough to ask, not just for a good day or a better life, but for the *impossible*. Then step forward to act in audacious faith.

Each of us is called to be a Joshua—each in our own way, in our own circumstances, with our own God-given personality. As you'll see in the pages ahead, you and I are called not just to *have* faith but also to regularly *activate* our faith by asking God for giant outcomes, taking giant steps. If we have the audacity to ask, God has the ability to perform. That's how God turns his amazing promises into everyday reality in every generation—for Joshua's and for ours.

You and I may not see the same miracles Joshua did, but we serve the same God. His nature never changes. The same power that stopped the sun and raised Christ from the grave lives in every believer. God still demonstrates his power and supplies his provision in direct proportion to the faith of his children.

Don't get me wrong. Audacious faith is not about throwing yourself off the top of a mountain and expecting God to catch you. It's not about thinking you can get God in your back pocket so that you can manipulate him for your own purposes. And— thank God—it's not about entering a gifted and talented program for the spiritually elite.

Audacious faith is for schoolteachers. Stay-at-home moms. Seventh-grade girls. (Seventh-grade boys too. Maybe.) Construction workers, bankers, hairstylists, college students. I've seen the sun stand still for all of them, and I'll share many of their stories with you.

Choosing to live with Sun Stand Still faith will never be the easiest way to live. In fact, it's often downright intimidating. But it's the best way to live. And if you're going to be a part of what God is doing in this generation, it's the *only* way to live.

It's time to write your own Sun Stand Still story. To pray your own Sun Stand Still prayers. And to live with audacious faith that expects the impossible to come to pass.

To the best of my ability, I'll show you how to do just that. Together we can be part of a great move of God in our generation.

I am a Joshua. And I am just like you.

CHAPTER 3

Page 23 Vision

I was sixteen when I gave my life to Christ. Before that, I was a pretty likable, relatively well-behaved Methodist kid, raised by good parents in a terrific small town. I used to wish I had a more dramatic testimony. You know the kind?

"Before I met Christ, I was the chief of sinners. At age six I fed crack cocaine to my dog. At age nine I began to experiment with heroin. By age nineteen I had been in and out of three maximum-security prisons. Years later, while leading an international witch-craft convention, I finally met Jesus…"

Sorry. That's not my story. And I want to point out that while some Christian conversion stories may be more spectacular than others, that doesn't make them any more significant. God gives people the exact experiences he wants them to have in order to shape the specific destiny he's designed for them. In fact, I can look back at my early life and see how God was forming an audacious vision in my life.

He's been doing the same thing in your life all along too. Granted, it can be hard to connect all the dots. And sometimes the best way to discern what God wants to do in your life is to hear about the discovery process in someone else's life. So let me share a little about how God gave a small-town boy like me a big-time vision.

Somehow all my exposure to the gospel never hit the spot and deeply transformed me until my junior year of high school. A friend invited me to revival services at a local Baptist church. The first night I went, I thought it was dreadfully boring. The best thing that came out of that night was the free meal afterward. And not just because it was free. At that dinner I became acquainted with someone who struck me as a different species of Christian. He was about my age and his name was Jody. I liked him immediately because he paid for my meal—and because he seemed absolutely authentic.

Over the course of several late-night conversations, Jody helped me embrace a true faith in Jesus Christ. And on one of the very last nights of the revival, I gave my life to Jesus the old-school way. I raised my hand and made the trek down to the front of the First Baptist Church. All the way from the balcony. I was making it official: "I choose to be a radical follower of Jesus Christ. And I'm not ashamed to be identified with him."

I see Jody as the sickle in my salvation process. My mom, my Sunday school teachers, and my grandfather—and God knows how many other people across the span of sixteen years—planted seeds and watered the ground. Jody was there to help reap the harvest. And God was the One who gave the increase.

My passions were redirected immediately and substantially. I had no drug addictions to shake, but I had a lot of attitudes and habits to exchange. I began to devour the New Testament and tell my pot-smoking friends about Jesus, often against their will. I'd take them to Taco Bell under false pretenses and then launch into a memorized presentation of the gospel from the book of Romans. I had even learned a closing technique that involved drawing a cross that bridged the gap between heaven and hell on a napkin. Most of the subjects listened politely and then got hammered at the keg party that weekend anyway. A few gave their lives to Christ and joined my crusade. I got high off every encounter, slipping into an evangelism addiction that I have never recovered from.

Later I would realize that all of this was just the prologue to the specific mission God had for my life. And it wasn't long before God started planting in my brain a long-term vision of the way he wanted to use me to make an impact on the world.

My vision was the catalyst of audacious faith: a personal, God-appointed dream or calling. I call it a Page 23 vision. You've got to have one if you're going to attempt the impossible. Yet many Christians are either completely oblivious to the concept or are content to settle for so much less.

I'm so glad God gave me my Page 23 vision early in life. It's just about the most valuable spiritual asset I've ever discovered.

The Sentence That Ruined My Life

A few months after my commitment to Christ, someone slipped me a book called *Fresh Wind, Fresh Fire* by a pastor in Brooklyn named Jim Cymbala. It was the first Christian book I ever willfully read. And it read like a highlight reel of the miracles God had performed in Cymbala's church. Addictions broken. Families restored. Souls saved. A city illuminated. I was mesmerized.

As I sat at my parents' kitchen table with the open book, hands still wet from washing the dishes, I stumbled across a line that set the trajectory of my life. It was on page 23:

> I despaired at the thought that my life might slip by without seeing God show himself mightily on our behalf.

It's hard to put into words how tightly that one sentence gripped my imagination. Somehow the Holy Spirit translated that line into a tangible impression in my teenage heart, and I knew: one day I'm going to start a church in a big city to reach people who are far from God.

Those words in the Cymbala book set off a nuclear reaction in my sixteen-year-old soul. In retrospect I can identify it as an epiphany. When I tell people about it now, I refer to it as my defining moment—my call to ministry. At the time, though, I felt only a strong impulse and a naive enthusiasm. I couldn't know what it would lead to. But in fact, everything would change.

See, up to this point, I'd had a pretty comfortable, mostly self-focused vision of what my life would be like. But page 23 ruined that vision. The seed of audacious faith in my heart had sprouted.

That's how your Page 23 vision is going to come to life. It will start with a seed of inspiration that takes root in your imagination. Over time, it will produce a harvest of obedience for the glory of God. And the whole process will take place deep in the soil of your faith.

I'm not saying a vision always starts with a sentence in a Christian book. I'm not saying it always hits you at a certain age. And—please don't miss this—I'm not suggesting that God gives only visions that are about starting a church or doing things we typically associate with ministry. In fact, in most cases, there is no lightning bolt and no connection to a religious profession. Usually, a Page 23 vision will begin when you see God dropping hints, not when you see him shooting stars in your direction. And your vision will probably flow from something you're already doing—relationships you've already established, priorities you're already passionate about.

The kind of vision that makes you bold enough to ask God for the impossible can come from many sources. It can materialize in a million ways. And it will mature over time, not in the blink of an eye.

But the bottom line is this: If you're going to ask God to do something impossible in your life, you've got to have some clarity about what you're asking for. You've got to know you're not just spinning a fantasy or going on a delusional ego trip. That's not the kind of unlimited potential we're talking about here. Far too many well-meaning Christians have wrecked their lives because they chased after a far-fetched idea that they sincerely thought came from God. And they would be the first to tell you to be careful that you don't mistake a delusion for a true vision. Both can make you see things that no one else sees.

If the dream in your heart isn't biblically based, focused on Jesus, affirmed by the key people in your life, and tethered to your passions, gifts, and life experiences, chances are, you're way off prompt.

The best way to avoid being duped by a counterfeit is to make sure you're familiar with the real thing. So what's *your* real thing? What's the impossible situation that God wants to make possible in your life? Is it a relationship he wants to repair? a weakness that he wants to help you overcome? someone who is far from God and who needs to be reached through your bold example?

something from your past that needs to be exchanged for the potential of your future? some need in the world that you are uniquely positioned to meet?   *YES*

I can't tell you exactly what your Page 23 vision will look like. Even if I could, I wouldn't. Doing so would cheat you out of the opportunity to know Christ more deeply. Discovering God's vision for your life is one of the primary ways God teaches you about his character. Seizing his big purpose for your life is not just about figuring out what God wants from you and getting down to business. It's also about becoming intimately acquainted with who Jesus is. It's about mining the depths of who you are in him. And out of that revelation, you will fulfill the purpose that he put you on the earth to fulfill.

Accomplishing the impossible is all about seeing the invisible.

Page 23 Profiles

Here are a few real-life examples of people with Page 23 visions. Maybe one of these profiles will help your own imagination percolate.

✳ My friend Matthew has a Page 23 vision. He's not a preacher. He's a businessman. And God has made him really good at investment strategies. So he's decided to systematically earn and return millions of dollars for the kingdom of God. He's extremely generous to his church, and he funds missionaries all over the world. He takes his checkbook everywhere he goes. When he sees a need, he prays about it. If he senses God's prompting, he writes a check on the spot.

He tears up every time he talks about his audacious faith. He tells me how much fun he's having by living with his eyes open to opportunities to make eternal investments every day. And he tells me about how much more he wants to give. His vision gives him a reason to get up in the morning, and it keeps him going when he has to work late into the night.

✴ Coach Brown has a Page 23 vision. He's the head football coach and athletic director at the high school where I graduated. Now, in my hometown, football isn't an extracurricular activity. It's more like a belief system. So you know Coach Brown is a VIP in Moncks Corner, South Carolina.

Coach Brown gave his life to Jesus around the same time I did. Only he wasn't sixteen years old. He was fifty. A lot of pride had built up in his life during a half century of living for himself. But soon everyone could tell that his heart was brand-new. His desires were born again. And the whole town watched his approach to life change because of his newfound vision.

At first, he so desperately wanted to make a difference for God that he thought a career change might be in order. But then he realized that no preacher in town could possibly have a pulpit more prominent than that of a football coach. He was perfectly positioned to shine for Christ by living with integrity, investing in his players, and of course winning games. I've talked to dozens of students who say they would have dropped out of school if it hadn't been for Coach Brown. Now they're committed Christians— and attending major universities on scholarships.

Coach Brown has left a legacy of transformation in his wake. Everyone in Moncks Corner knows what he stands for. Even if they don't agree with his beliefs, they respect him. After all, not only is he a good man, but he also just gave the town its third state championship title.

✳ Kelly has a Page 23 vision. She's a part of a group of high-school seniors I meet with regularly. I teach them the Bible, answer their questions about following Christ, and challenge them to dream big for God's glory.

I usually open the meeting by inviting a few of them to share what the Lord is doing in their lives. One particular day, Kelly could hardly wait to talk when I called on her. She wanted to let me know that she had experienced the beginnings of her own Page 23 vision.

I asked her what it was. She said she finally realized that, all her life, she had been fascinated with filmmaking. I asked her if she was any good at it. Some of the kids in the group said that, yes, she was really good. I asked what she was going to do to keep getting better. She said she's going to school to study filmmaking. But she's not just going to make a career out of it—she's also embracing it as her calling. She wants to be a part of making movies that will have a deep impact on the culture. I asked her how she's going to quantify her impact. She replied, without a shred of arrogance or pretense, "Maybe when I win an Academy Award?"

Nobody in the room laughed. Kelly wasn't kidding. Her vision is all business.

Maybe Kelly is naive. But maybe we all need to be more than a little naive if we're really going to be used by God.

Sanctified Naiveté

After the initial detonation of my Page 23 vision, God kept confirming my passion to move to a major metropolitan area to start a church. But here's the thing: I knew nothing about big cities. My hometown had a population of six thousand people, and some folks considered a trip to Wal-Mart an event to get all dressed up for. I knew even less about starting a church. Certainly I felt way too young to take on such a serious task that required this much wisdom. But somehow I sensed that none of this would matter. Ignorance and inexperience wouldn't count as valid excuses. When God speaks, he does not stutter. When he awakens you to your calling, the snooze button stops working. It was time for me to get busy for God.

I soon discovered that when the scope of your vision seems a lot bigger than your base of knowledge or breadth of experience, you're in good company. God grabbed hold of a lot of my favorite Bible characters when they were pretty young too. Jeremiah explained to God that he was too young to speak out as a prophet. God made him a counteroffer and told him to do it anyway. Timothy apparently had misgivings about his maturity level. Paul told him to stop making excuses and start leading by example.

This may sound presumptuous, but I think I know why God gave me a bold vision for my life at such a young age. He had to get to me before I was old enough to know any better. See, audacious faith starts with sanctified naiveté. There's an unquestioning optimism that comes as standard equipment when you're young. Honestly, I think it's a gift from God. Time can talk you out of your dreams. Routine can weaken your propensity toward audacity.

But believe me: It's never too late for you to embrace an audacious vision for your life. Read Joshua 14 about how Joshua's comrade Caleb was still driving out giants and taking mountains when he was eighty-five years old. Don't think for a moment that bold vision is reserved for the next generation. As you'll discover throughout this book, audacity does not discriminate on the basis of age or disqualify because of wasted years. No matter how far behind you feel, or how many opportunities you've squandered, you can begin to ask God to do the impossible in your life right now.

When you examine the lives of people who are called to do great things for God, regardless of their age, you'll usually notice three things:

✳ They offer God a long list of excuses.

✳ God doesn't seem surprised.

✳ God doesn't change his mind.

I point this out because the moment you start developing your Page 23 vision, your old way of thinking will try to demolish it. Your mind will be flooded with all the reasons why it will never work. You'll remember all the times you've tried to do something great before—and failed miserably.

But audacious vision never cowers in the darkness. The darker it gets, the brighter our faith can shine. Audacious faith takes Jesus at his word. We are the light of the world: we cannot be hidden—and we have no reason to hide (Matthew 5:14).

The legions of the naive can change reality just by being ready to respond to the visions God gives them.

SEIZING THE VISION

There's a prayer I pray almost every day over both of my sons. Most nights I slip into their rooms after they're sound asleep, place my right hand just barely on their heads, and whisper: "God, raise up my sons to be the greatest men of God of their generation." Of course I share my prayer with them when they're awake too. But they're preschoolers. They don't exactly respond with, "I receive this prophetic blessing from you, Dad, the patriarch of my lineage, in the name of the living Christ." In other words, I highly doubt they get it. But one day they will. I'm just trying to stock their hearts with raw material that God can use to build a vision within my boys when they're older. Maybe the sentence I'm praying will ruin their lives the same way the sentence on page 23 of Jim Cymbala's book ruined my life. Maybe it will be the genesis of their own Sun Stand Still prayers.

Now, if you have kids who happen to be the same age as mine and you'd like to pray this same prayer for them, too bad. You'll have to modify it. Your son will have to settle for the title of Second Greatest Man of God. (Of course, Greatest Woman of God is still available.)

I'm kidding, of course. There's no gold medal event going on here. But I'm dead serious about the sentiment. Audacity plays to win. I don't want to raise good boys. I want to raise great men who will do great things for a great God. I once heard a preacher say in a sermon, "I'm not raising my kids to survive the world. I'm raising them to change it." I've adopted that mantra as my own. I encourage you to think the same way.

I'm not telling you any of this so that you'll be impressed by what a great dad I am. Actually, the point I'm trying to make has very little to do with me and my boys. It has everything to do with you and your vision. If you haven't made the personal connection yet, let me give it to you straight:

* **Seize.** If you want to see God do something impossible in your life, you've got to open your heart and mind to God's vision for your life.
* **Activate.** Audacious faith starts when you choose to step out in a strength not your own. Pursuing God's larger purpose for your life will propel you to pray audacious Sun Stand Still prayers.
* **Make your move.** And when you act boldly on God's supernatural answers, you'll find yourself in the middle of a move of God.

Before Joshua could change the world through audacious faith, he had to seize God's vision in a Page 23 moment of his own. Technically, it wasn't on page 23. It's actually located in Joshua 1:2–5:

> Moses my servant is dead. Now then, you and all these people, get ready to cross the Jordan River into the land I am about to give to them—to the Israelites. I will give you every place where you set your foot, as I promised Moses. Your territory will extend from the desert to Lebanon, and from the great river, the Euphrates—all the Hittite country—to the Great Sea on the west. No one will be able to stand up against you all the days of your life. As I was with

Moses, so I will be with you; I will never leave you nor forsake you.

It doesn't get much clearer than that. First, God told Joshua to believe that through God's power he would be able to do the impossible, as he showed him the specific vision he intended Joshua to accomplish. Next, he instructed Joshua to activate his faith by taking bold, courageous steps based on the promises of God. And in radical obedience, Joshua went on to lead his nation in one of the most stunning military upsets in history.

In a nutshell, this is the progression of Sun Stand Still faith: Seize God's vision. Activate your faith. Make your move.

How much different would things be if you started living this way right now? Isn't it a phenomenal proposition? Here's what's even more astonishing: this kind of faith doesn't just change *you,* it also enables you to be a part of *changing the world.*

Imagine with me: How radically different would modern American youth culture be if we stopped raising our kids to survive their world and started empowering them with a vision to change it? How much more stable and unified would the economic and political landscape of our world become if all of us were guided by vision, regardless of our ages or stations in life? How would your general outlook shift if you woke up every morning, not just to a to-do list, but to goals and activities that flowed from a Page 23 vision?

Seizing God's vision means deciding that you will not spend another day surviving your work environment, family dynamic, or dysfunctional situation. Instead, you will bring about substantial change for the glory of God. That's the heart of a Page 23 vision. That's a purpose you can build your faith on.

Without a Page 23 vision, I would have gone buck wild as a teenager. I would have gone on my senior cruise and gotten wasted instead of leading my youth group on a missions trip to one of the poorest counties in our state.

Without a Page 23 vision, I wouldn't have saved my virginity for my wife, let alone waited to kiss her for the first time on our wedding day.

Without a Page 23 vision, I wouldn't have had the courage to ignore the opinions of those who insisted that it couldn't be done when I started sharing publicly what God was calling me to do with my life.

Without a Page 23 vision, I won't have what it takes to maintain purity and integrity for the next fifty years as a husband, father, and pastor. My calling is great, the stakes are high, and stellar character is required. My vision defines the parameters that I live by.

The same is true for you.

Without a Page 23 vision, you'll settle into survival mode. You'll feel like a spiritual failure because you'll constantly compare yourself to others instead of looking to Jesus. You'll try to manage your sins and behave like a good little Christian instead of dreaming big dreams, stepping out in great faith, and reflecting the greatness of God.

Our sinful behaviors won't be reined in by more rules and regulations. Rules without revelation result in rebellion. Audacious faith demands much more than self-control. It is the spin-off of future hope. You've got to have a Page 23 promise to call your own.

No, you're not Joshua. You don't get to apply for an internship with Moses. That program is closed for enrollment. But you have a personal birthright to believe in a God-given mission for your life. And if God can instill and fulfill a big-city dream of enormous Kingdom impact in a small-town boy like me, he can put a Sun Stand Still spirit in you too.

Consider this your page 23.

CHAPTER 4

The Sun Stand Still Lexicon

Before we go any further in this experience together, I want to clarify some keywords and phrases that we've already encountered and that will continue to appear throughout the book. It's not that I question your intelligence, but I come at these concepts from a unique angle, and I want us to be on the same page about them. Otherwise, I'll say one thing and you might hear another.

Here they are...

Sun Stand Still Prayer

As you've already discovered, Sun Stand Still is based on a prayer in Joshua 10 that affected time and space. If you choose to interpret the Bible literally on this point (as I do), God *actually made the day longer* to reveal his glory in response to a specific prayer that Joshua prayed.

As it applies to you, Sun Stand Still is a metaphor for the seemingly impossible things God wants to do in and through your life. A Sun Stand Still prayer applies audacious faith to a clearly defined need or goal that requires God's supernatural involvement.

Critical clarification: A Sun Stand Still prayer is appropriate for any area of your life that is in alignment with God's will. In other words, Sun Stand Still prayers aren't for selfish purposes, but neither are they only for the spiritual stuff. Here are some of the most common things I've seen people pray Sun Stand Still prayers about:

* broken relationships
* financial provision
* career aspirations
* spiritual breakthroughs at work, in the community, or elsewhere in the world
* physical and emotional healing
* loved ones who are far from God
* standing strong against temptation
* achieving important life goals
* finding and embracing purpose
* ministry resources and momentum

Page 23 Vision

Before you can pray a Sun Stand Still prayer, asking God to do the impossible, you've got to set your sights on the specific impossible thing God wants you to trust him for in *your* life.

That can happen only when you see and seize God's vision for your life. When I use the word *vision,* I mean "a clear sense of purpose regarding what God wants to do through your life." Some people would refer to it as a calling or a life mission. As we saw in chapter 3, I call it a Page 23 vision.

Whatever you call it, you've got to have it. Believing God for the impossible begins with seeing the invisible—understanding who God is and what he wants to accomplish through you. The

Sun Stand Still prayers you pray will often be temporary and specific in nature. But they will always flow from God's overarching vision for your life.

Critical clarification: This message isn't for leaders only. It's for everybody. So I'm not going to limit us to the kind of applications normally associated with vision—for example, running an organization or developing long-term strategies. I'm simply trying to help you locate the pulse of God's will for your life so you can begin to believe him *in extraordinary ways*.

The opposite of Page 23 vision: survival mode.

Impossible

In this book we're learning to believe God for the impossible. So, what qualifies as impossible? Anything that seems impossible to you.

If there's a relationship in your life that seems damaged beyond repair, that qualifies as a personal impossibility for you.

If there's a goal that you believe God is leading you to set, and you know you can't do it apart from him, it's totally appropriate to refer to that as an impossibility. Even though someone else might be able to accomplish it easily, it's impossible for *you*. And God relates to each of us uniquely.

Or let's say there's a temptation you can't seem to shake. All your life you've felt powerless to overcome it. Eventually you may begin to feel as if achieving victory in this area of your life is impossible. You're not implying that it can't be done or even that it's never been done before. You mean that you are completely dependent on God's strength to obtain the freedom you need. That's a good thing.

Critical clarification: In the strictest sense of the term, impossibilities don't exist, because there's absolutely nothing our God can't do (Matthew 19:26; Luke 1:37). But each of us has dreams and possibilities that lie beyond our human reasoning and abilities. And audacious faith, activated by your Sun Stand Still prayer, is the channel God uses to override your impossibilities with his power. "Everything is possible for him who believes" (Mark 9:23).

The opposite of impossible: the ordinary.

Audacity

I realize a term like *audacity* can come across like empty jargon. And some may mistake *audacity* as a synonym for *cockiness* or *arrogance*. That's unfortunate. But we're not going to abandon the terminology. Instead, we're going to redeem it. Trust me: the kind of audacity I'm dealing is good stuff, and you're going to want plenty of it.

Biblical audacity is a mind-set that approaches God with confidence and believes him for the impossible. It's rooted in the gospel and it's powered by the Holy Spirit. The Scriptures are saturated with examples and teachings about audacity, so it will be impossible for us to get to all of them. But you'll get the gist.

Critical clarification: Audacity is not an *activity*. Audacity is an *approach*. Audacity isn't qualified by *what* you do. It's all about *how* you do what you do. So you don't have to be a third-world missionary to have audacity. Audacity is every bit as attainable for you, whether you are a stay-at-home mom or an electrical engineer—if you dare to relate to God on a new level.

The opposite of audacity: complacency.

Audacious Faith

Since this is a book about believing God for the impossible, the nucleus of our message is *faith.* You can't please God without it (Hebrews 11:6). You can't be saved apart from it (Ephesians 2:8). But way too many Christians have a distorted view of it.

Unfortunately, faulty interpretations of isolated verses have resulted in shaky foundations of faith for many Christians. Honestly, it's hard to know where to start deconstructing the myths.

Listen, there are entire volumes of theology written by brilliant scholars who attempt to define every nuance of faith. This isn't one of them. For the purposes of this book, when I talk about faith, I'm mainly referring to a certain kind of faith. I call it audacious faith. It describes an attitude and a set of actions that are deeply rooted in, even required by, your conviction that all things are possible with God.

Audacious faith isn't some newfangled, extrabiblical variety of faith. It's a return to the core of Christianity: trusting Jesus completely in every area of your life and setting out to devote your life wholly to revealing his glory in this world.

Critical clarification: We are saved by grace through faith in Christ—period. Don't look at the challenge to act in audacious faith as an add-on to this saving faith. It's a call to press *deeper* into that faith, until it becomes more and more effective in your everyday life.

The opposite of audacious faith: passive unbelief.

A Move of God / The Miraculous

I always hesitate to toss around phrases like *move of God* or words like *miracle.* It seems to cheapen the meaning of the word *miraculous* when you use it to describe everything from the parting of the Red Sea to the selling of your house at asking price.

So let's be clear about this: according to the Bible, God has performed miracles throughout history that have defied natural laws—the resurrection of the dead and the stopping of the sun, to name a couple. I believe God is still able to do these types of things today, and testimonies from believers all over the world substantiate my claim.

But in this book we're broadening our view of God's miraculous intervention to include the affairs of our everyday lives.

When I talk about a *miracle* or a *move of God* (I use the terms interchangeably), I'm not necessarily referring to a supernatural phenomenon from a scientific perspective. I'm more focused on the way God's power infuses the life of ordinary believers to produce results that glorify Jesus. Sometimes these miracles are tangible and remarkable. Other times they're hidden and more subtle.

Either way, any time our heavenly Father intersects our earthly lives and answers our prayers by any means he chooses, it's a miraculous occurrence. And I believe he desires to do this in a bigger way in our lives—here and now—than most of us have ever imagined.

*

Now I want to put all these key terms together to show you—in one declaration—what you can expect from this book:

Your *Sun Stand Still prayer,*
based on your *Page 23 vision,*
activated by *audacious faith,*
will mark your life by the *miraculous,*
empower you to achieve the *impossible,*
and put you in the middle of a *move of God.*

I think you've got it.
Let's keep moving...

CHAPTER 5

Ignite the Ordinary

I can sense your objections: *Audacious faith comes naturally when you're the pastor of a big church. Not all of us have that advantage, Furtick. It's harder to believe the sun could stand still when you're forty-three years old and work in the accounting department. Where's the opportunity for audacity in that?*

When we hear about the big things God is doing through others, it can make our own achievements and assignments seem small. I know that all too well. When we started Elevation, I attended leadership conferences as part of my search for affirmation and validation. But listening to one Super Pastor after another often left me discouraged and burdened by insecurities. It seemed like they had more people on their custodial staff than I had in my entire church. Clearly, God does special things in a special way through special people. But where does that leave the rest of us?

Right now, you might be thinking that nothing remarkable—much less supernatural—ever happens to you. Your prayers appear to be rarely and randomly answered. And no agenda item in your life seems big enough to warrant God's undivided attention anyway. Audacity seems to be reserved exclusively for others—the *special* Christians. Comparing your achievements to those of the best and the brightest can leave you feeling like a complete failure.

Maybe your extraordinary neighbor is stressed because his latest promotion landed him in a much higher tax bracket. Ordinary you is well on your way to an ulcer because you just maxed out a third credit card.

The extraordinary moms in the soccer league can't decide which elite private school would be ideal for their third grader. Ordinary you can barely afford to keep your third grader playing soccer, let alone rescue him from the perils of—*gasp!*—public school.

An extraordinary someone you know, with a net worth much lower than yours, has a sense of purpose much higher than any you've ever experienced. Ordinary you feels empty, your earnings and accomplishments don't help, and you're not getting any younger. You feel as if time is running out.

The ache of the ordinary is so common that many Christians settle for taking sedatives to numb the pain instead of pursuing treatment to cure the condition. But here's what I know: God is able to stir up your spirit, pour out his presence, and reveal his glory in your family, business, or community. And in this chapter I want to show you that the extraordinary presence and purpose of God will burn brightly in the life of anyone willing to be set on fire.

Unlikely Encounters in the Boondocks

When you strip the biblical miracles of their spectacular special effects, a common plot point emerges: extraordinary moves of God begin with ordinary acts of obedience. That singular fact gives you a starting place. It doesn't matter who you are or what you do for a living. If God lives in you, you have the potential for audacious faith. I'm pretty certain that Joshua grasped this fact from the very first days of his working partnership with Moses. His mentor was at the center of some of the most extraordinary feats ever recorded in the Bible. Yet it all began with an ordinary day's work.

Moses' first encounter with God is recorded in Exodus 3. The way their meeting goes down should be extremely encouraging for anyone who has ever felt stuck doing average stuff in a distant place.

The setting is the far side of the desert.

Moses is tending sheep.

The sheep belong to Moses' father-in-law.

A bush catches on fire.

Moses walks over to look…

(Sarcasm alert.) This screenplay is bound to start bidding wars all over Hollywood. What audience wouldn't be riveted by a scene like this? And as for Moses, who wouldn't accept a leading role of this magnitude?

In reality, when you peel back the layers, the illustrious burning bush encounter that seemed so captivating in Sunday school is really quite…ordinary. Moses is performing menial manual labor. Working for his father-in-law. Does it get any more mundane?

Almost all encounters with God begin that way. You may be living under the illusion that when God ignites great things in your life, he'll announce it with a big bang. He might. It's more likely that he won't. So stop waiting around for the big bang. Pay attention to the subtle clues and the still, small voice. God lives in that place too.

Even on the day the sun stood still, an ordinary event paved the way for an extraordinary victory. After all, the sun shines all the time. That's ordinary. But only God can make it shine for a full extra day. That's extraordinary. What we call a miracle is really just the right combination of your ordinary ingredients and God's extraordinary expertise. And when God's super collides with your natural, sparks will fly:

* God may allow you to receive a negative report from the doctor. Ordinary. But you trust him in a way that causes all your close friends to see Christ clearly through your response. Extraordinary.

* God may call you to serve as an unsung youth pastor of fifteen kids, leading meetings in a moldy basement, with an Atari for entertainment. Ordinary. But he may also be providing you with the opportunity to pour your life into one of those teenagers who will go on to preach the gospel in a thousand places you'll never go. Extraordinary.

* God may lead you to stay at home with your young children, forfeiting a second income. Ordinary. But along with diapers, dishes, and naps, you receive the gift of time—to model discipline, instill values, and speak life into your kids. They could grow up to be Joshuas in their own generation. Extraordinary.

* God may have placed you in a line of work that seems to have no eternal value and provides very little in the way of personal fulfillment. Ordinary. But he knows you're the only Christian witness many of your co-workers and clients will ever meet. They'll observe what God looks like as you labor with excellence and integrity every day. Extraordinary.

Look around your desert today. It might be your office, your living room, your church, your neighborhood, your classroom. If God is calling you to make a big difference, he usually starts in a small way—a flaming bush that only you will notice.

Will you remove your shoes, draw close, and receive your assignment? Will you give the Lord permission to ignite your ordinary? If you will, I promise it won't be long before your faith starts carrying you to a level higher than you ever thought you could go.

ORDINARY GEORGE

George certainly never thought he'd end up leading a team of volunteers to Haiti just weeks after the January 2010 earthquake flattened the capital city. George is not a missionary. He's an orthopedic physician's assistant who wants his life to count for Christ. But he decided a few years ago to stop waiting around for God to issue a dramatic call for him to do something great. Instead, he made the decision to put his skills to work for Jesus at a moment's notice.

Specifically, he prays for God to use him in the life of everyone he meets. And when God opens a door, George walks through it. A pretty simple strategy actually. But the results are supernatural.

George is one of those rare believers who goes to work on the lookout for burning bushes every day. He doesn't sign every cast with a Bible verse and an ichthus. He doesn't share the gospel while he's supposed to be relocating a shoulder. He just goes about the routine stuff with an attitude that invites God to nudge him anytime, anywhere. When George sees a patient, you can tell he's doing more than crossing a name off the list.

There's just something different about George. Ask anyone who knows him. Actually, you don't have to ask anyone else. I can give you a firsthand account.

I don't know quite what to make of this, but my three-year-old, Graham, has busted his head open two times in the last year. In the exact same spot on his forehead. Once he fell on the bathtub. The next time he fell on the coffee table. Both times his big brother swore it was an accident and seemed to feel really bad about pushing him.

It's terrifying to see your kid's face covered with blood. And that's usually followed by the fun of hanging out in the emergency room waiting to get stitches. But when you're George's pastor, George doesn't let you wait for hours with your son in the emergency room. He insists that you see him right away. He meets you in the parking lot (on the night of the Super Bowl— bad timing, boys), gives you a hug, and tells your son he's going to take good care of him. Even the second time around, when your son is hesitant because he remembers that this is the man who recently came at him with sharp objects, George has a way of setting him—and everyone else—at ease. In fact, in a span of about thirty minutes, Graham went from describing George as "the man who's gonna hurt me" to giving George a hug and telling him, "I love you, Dr. George."

I'm telling you, there's something special about George. It's not his IQ that sets him apart, although he's a bright guy. He doesn't have a forceful personality. He might never deliver a speech to a packed house. I've heard him sing, and I'm definitely not inviting him to sing a solo anytime soon. (Sorry, George.) But George is completely available to Jesus. And as he has increased his spiritual availability through unconditional obedience, more of God's power has become available to him. That's how he recently found the courage to assemble a team of twenty other medical professionals to carry forty-three army duffel bags of medical supplies to Haiti.

The Red Cross didn't call George and ask him for his services. The church didn't schedule an official missions trip. No independently wealthy philanthropist offered to pay George's way and fund the trip for all the volunteers. Like millions of other people, George just watched the news. But unlike most other people, he did more than watch. He processed what was happening in human terms, asked God what he should do, and then took a step of obedience. And then another step. And another. Until he found himself serving in some of the most desolate circumstances in recent history, seeing some of the most miraculous results a Christian could ever hope to witness.

You should hear how fast George gets going when he's telling the stories. Extraordinary stories. Like the one about how they left Santo Domingo on a bus pulling a trailer carrying twenty-two hundred pounds of medical supplies. Six hours later, they made their first stop and realized the trailer was missing. It had come detached from the bus—they had no idea where. They prayed that the trailer was undamaged and the supplies were untouched. And after they turned around and drove back to the place they came from, they found the trailer sitting upright at a military checkpoint untouched, with several armed Dominican soldiers guarding it.

Or the extraordinary story about a three-year-old named Bernard who had never spoken a word to anyone. On the last day of the trip, George and his team were called to help Bernard, who was sitting on a wooden bench outside a clinic. They began the surgery to free the boy's tongue. At one point, when Bernard got restless, one of the physicians began singing "Jesus Loves Me" in his ear. Soon all the team members and fifty or so orphans watching the surgery joined in. A specialist named Bobby finished the procedure while tears flowed from his eyes. Bernard gave everyone a laugh as he stuck out his tongue. George tells me: "Our Sun Stand Still prayer is that Bernard will one day become a pastor and preach the gospel in Haiti."

Ordinary George will carry the extraordinary memories of those miraculous moments for the rest of his life. And I don't believe he's supposed to be the exception. This is the kind of blessing that God longs to pour out on all of us if only we'll get serious about using everything we've got for his glory.

CONNECTOR TO THE CURRENT

There are certain phrases I'd like to see permanently banned from our Christian vocabulary. The one that sets me off the most is *full-time ministry.* I know what it's supposed to mean, but I vehemently disagree with its implications. To say that someone is called to full-time ministry suggests that others are permitted to do part-time ministry. But Jesus didn't die on a part-time cross. He doesn't love us with a part-time love. He doesn't cover us with a part-time pardon for sins. There's no such thing as a part-time Christian, and there's no such thing as part-time ministry.

The day you gave your life to Christ, you signed a full-time ministry employee agreement. A very small percentage of Christians derive their livelihood from a religious institution, so it's very likely that you work in the educational, legal, medical, financial, or some other industry. But no matter who pays your salary, you're a full-time employee of the kingdom of God. And wherever you work, that's your ministry. Whatever you're good at, that's your calling. The components of your assignment are the sources of your significance. And there are burning bushes all around you. Every business negotiation is an opportunity for Christ to shine through you. Every teachable moment with your children is a bright spot in the making. Everywhere you set your foot is potential holy ground. And this concept is the key to effectiveness in the local church.

I teach our people at Elevation that the day I became their pastor, I left the "ministry." I'm pretty sure Rick Warren said it before me, and I'm completely sure the apostle Paul said it before him. Ephesians 4:11–12 explains that the only job pastors and teachers have is to prepare God's people for their own personal ministry. So if the people don't have a ministry, I don't have a job. The people in my church aren't just season ticket holders. They don't fill the seats to watch my exegetical dunking skills. I refuse to limit our impact by becoming a one-man show. And when the preacher is a ball hog, it robs others of the opportunity to express their gifts and give their service as an act of worship.

I want the people in our church to see themselves as marketplace missionaries. They are the image of God within their spheres of influence.

And when it comes to the ministry of the local church, I believe every member is a link in the chain of the life-change process. In fact, they're so much more than that. I tell all my volunteers at Elevation Church that they are connectors to the current of the power of Christ: the grace of Christ flows through them into the lives of those they serve.

So we have a couple thousand volunteers who make Elevation

Church happen week after week. There's a place for everyone to jump in and serve. Our purpose statement is: *So that people far from God will be filled with life in Christ.* And our volunteers get it. They understand that they are a vital part of changing lives.

At least most of them do.

One day I overheard a volunteer greeting a visitor in our offices. The volunteer seemed peppy and capable: "Hi! Welcome to Elevation! How can we help you?"

Listening from around the corner, I mused: *What a sharp lady. She gets it.* But what she said next made me wonder.

"Do you work here?" the guest asked.

My dear, sweet, misguided volunteer replied, "No, I'm just a volunteer."

Just a volunteer? Just a volunteer? I wanted to scream. *You're not just a volunteer! You've never been and will never be just a volunteer. You are a connector to the current of the power of Christ.*

Okay, maybe I'm reading too much into this woman's word choice. Technically, she was just trying to say that she's not on the payroll. But still, the church needs to bury that "I'm just a volunteer" mentality in a tomb. Let me explain why.

You see, every weekend thousands of people show up at Elevation. Hundreds of them are first-time guests. And many give their lives to Christ. This happens after we sing songs and I preach a message. So it stands to reason that the music and the sermon led to their salvation experience, right? It's not quite that simple.

Ultimately, Jesus saves people through the Holy Spirit. But he does it through much broader means than only what happens up on the platform.

There's the person who stepped out of her comfort zone to invite the guest to come to church with her. There are the parking lot attendants in orange vests waving batons and smiling, helping the visitor to find a parking spot, making him feel at ease. At the entryways and doors, there is an unusually happy army of greeters, all expressing the same sentiment: *This church is the place to be...* The visitor's anticipation starts to build, whether he admits it or not. He realizes, *These people seem happy to be here. They seem happy I'm here. Maybe there's something to this Jesus thing after all.*

There are the ushers, escorts, youth ministers... I can't even keep track of all the roles, and I'm the pastor. But no matter what the specific job description, every single person I've described is a connector to the current of the power of Christ.

Before the first note is ever played for our first-time guest (let's call him Will), production volunteers have been up for hours, transforming the rented high school auditorium where we meet into a habitation for the presence of God. The guy who pulled the trailer at 4:30 a.m. and the girl who set up the cameras—they are connectors to the current of the power of Christ.

By the time I open my mouth to start the sermon, Christ has already been preached. When Will raises his hand to receive Christ after attending for three months, he may say that the songs and the sermons changed his life. But the real miracle happened outside the service, with hundreds of ordinary people doing ordinary things with extraordinary passion for the glory of God.

No act of service is insignificant when done for the most significant purpose in the universe: proclaiming the gospel of Jesus Christ. When you see yourself as a connector to the current of the power of Christ, everything you do takes on meaning. Ordinary and audacity cannot coexist. They are diametrically opposed and mutually exclusive. You're not *just* a normal Christian who is *just* a volunteer. You're not *just* a church member or *just* an employee. Wherever you are, whatever you're doing, you're a connector to the current of the power of Christ. You are a servant of the Most High God.

JESUS' AFFINITY FOR THE ORDINARY

So, why is it that so many believers default on their potential to see God do the impossible in their lives? I think a lot of Christians feel that they should leave the big stuff to the religious pros and celebrity pastors. They feel like they're doing their part as long as they live decent lives. Stay out of trouble. Pay taxes. Have babies. Make a living. Buy a boat. Hit age fifty-nine and a half. Collect retirement. Die.

This is an unacceptable existence for redeemed sons and daughters of the King. You've got to do better than that. With God's help, you *will* do better than that.

You might be thinking you're unimpressive and unqualified. That's good. God performs the most impressive feats through the most unimpressive people. God likes to wet the wood before he sets it on fire. That way, everybody knows who made it burn (1 Kings 18:33–38).

When Jesus' ministry opened for business, he enlisted ordinary people skilled in ordinary ways. Wouldn't a rabbinical school have made for a more appropriate disciple candidate pool than a family fishing business? There was no shortage of talent in the seminaries of Jesus' day, but he passed over the MDivs and scooped up a collection agent named Matthew.

And Jesus' affinity for the ordinary didn't stop with his selection process. Over the course of his three-year earthly ministry, most of his recorded miracles happened in the marketplace or by the side of the road, not in the synagogue. Put that in your theological pipe and take a toke. Your Sun Stand Still assignment might not be meteoric. It might be mundane. But when you give all you've got for the cause of the One who gave it all to you in the first place, the effects of your investment will literally reach the heavens.

The Ramen Noodle Revival

In my freshman year of college I saw the power of ordinary acts of obedience revealed...in my dorm. I attended a small Baptist college in South Carolina, where I ended up rooming with Jody— the same guy who had led me to Christ when I was sixteen. He also ended up becoming my brother-in-law. (I'm telling you, nothing just happens. When God superintends your decisions, ordinary events are connected in extraordinary ways.)

Jody and I were in an interesting position because the college decided to house us in the athletic dorm, on the third floor, with half the football team. What made it more interesting was the discovery that we were the only guys who claimed to be followers of Christ on the hall. And the only white boys to boot. And oh, the only ones who didn't play football. Do you remember this *Sesame Street* song?

> One of these things is not like the others,
> One of these things just doesn't belong.

The first few months of my freshman year felt a lot like that.

I certainly didn't resent being one of the only two white guys on the hall. I kind of relished it. After all, I had been the only white kid in the black gospel choir during my senior year of high school. So I was used to glowing in the dark. The value of diversity is in my DNA. Still, I was having a hard time finding common ground with these guys.

I had a passion to see them give their lives to Christ, but nothing in my win-people-to-Jesus playbook was working. I invited them to church, Bible study, and prayer meeting. But North Greenville University already required us to attend chapel two times a week. By the time Sunday rolled around, these gentlemen were all churched out. Plus, I was starting to sense that more awareness of the gospel wasn't the answer. They'd heard it all before. What they needed was a demonstration.

One night I had a revelation. It was a lot like the classic line in one of the classic movies of my childhood, starring one of the worst actors in American cinematography. You remember the recurring voice in *Field of Dreams:* "If you build it, he will come"? Well, I heard a voice kind of like that. Only it wasn't out loud, and the message was slightly different: *If you feed them, they will come.*

This was my freshman-year burning bush. I was going to feed these fellows into the kingdom of God.

I immediately got in my Toyota Tercel and hit the closest grocery store, which was twenty minutes away. (Our school really was in the middle of nowhere.) I filled the cart with groceries and almost emptied my bank account to pay for them. It was good stuff too—Little Debbie. Oatmeal Creme Pies. Honey Buns. Nutty Buddy Bars. And of course the nutritional staple of higher education: ramen noodles. Only the best for the cause of Christ. About a hundred bucks in groceries. That's a fortune for a college student.

I hustled back up to the third floor, cleared out the top of my closet, and stocked it like a pantry. Then I went door to door, only this time, instead of inviting the guys to church, I invited them back to my room. To eat my food. My new and improved pitch went something like this: "God put it on my heart to start giving away my food to anybody who wants it, anytime you need it. I'm in room 318, so anytime you're hungry, just stop by the room. I'll even leave the door unlocked. No strings attached."

My initiative was successful. Too successful. By the time I had knocked on every door on the hall and turned around to head back, I had a train of large African American football players following me back to the room to take me up on my offer. Within five minutes flat, they had cleaned me out. One hundred bucks in groceries gone. Just like that.

Jody turned to me and said with classic country-boy twang, "Well, that was real slick of ya. What you gonna do now, food pantry man?"

To tell you the truth, I hadn't thought that far ahead. I knew what I wasn't going to do: quit. I refused to give up that easily. I may have been a broke college student, but since God is loaded, I pressed on with the food ministry. And the Lord provided. Somehow, I always had enough food to give away. It wasn't five thousand men, five loaves, and two fish, but it was the closest thing to a multiplication miracle I'd ever experienced. The guys would regularly stop by the room to pick up some food, and some of them even asked me to pray for them.

But nothing extraordinary was happening. No one was repenting of sin, trusting Jesus, or even making obvious spiritual progress. So a few months in, hundreds of dollars and many processed foods later, I felt like maybe this bright idea had run its course. I had a conversation with God, explaining, *Lord, this is expensive. These cats are eating my food, but no one is getting saved. I really need someone to pray the sinner's prayer and give me a reason to keep this thing going. Otherwise, I'm going to shut this little food pantry down. Amen?*

A few nights later, just as Jody and I were falling asleep, someone knocked at the door. Honestly, my first reaction wasn't audacity. It was more like animosity. *It's almost midnight. Is someone really knocking at my door to ask for food at midnight?*

But this guy didn't want food. He wanted to talk about Jesus.

I was really shocked because, in some ways, he was the hardest, most resistant one on the hall. We called him D. And I would have voted him least likely to receive Jesus. Good thing God doesn't poll me for election purposes.

D sat down on our bean bag and opened up with this line: "Ya'll are crazy."

Thanks, man. Anything else?

"I mean, I've been at this school for three years now. Everybody has tried to tell me I need Jesus. But nobody has ever just given me their food. Ya'll are crazy. And being around ya'll crazy white boys, I'm starting to see it. I need God in my life."

If the idea to start the food pantry was my burning bush, this was my Mount Sinai. I closed in for the kill: "Okay, let's do this. You can give your life to Christ right here, right now."

D didn't accept my proposal.

"Naw, naw, man. I wanna do it the right way. In church this Sunday."

I broke it down theologically: "The church isn't a building or a program. The church is God's people. We're here; we're the church. Let's do this right now."

D didn't budge.

"I want to do it in church. The right way."

One more try. "What do you need, D? You need me to print a bulletin? Sing a song? Take an offering? Let's do this!"

D still wasn't feeling me. And he was bigger than I was.

So off to church we went that Sunday. Me, D, and three of the other football players. All packed into my Toyota Tercel. Even if I had to Fred Flintstone that thing up the hill, we were going to get there. D picked the church, and of course he chose a church where I'd be the only white face in the crowd, clapping off rhythm. Cool with me. I was used to that.

That day, during the invitation, D made his move. He walked the aisle, bowed his knee, and asked Jesus to come into his life. And all his friends were watching.

His change was sudden and dramatic. He started reading his Bible incessantly. In fact, his roommate was a little upset. He grilled me: "Steve, what have you done to my boy? He don't wanna go to the club or nothing. Just wanna sit around and read Matthew, Mark, Luke, and John...Matthew, Mark, Luke, and John."

Before long, that roommate gave his life to Christ too. Followed by one of the guys across the hall. Now the flywheel was spinning, and revival had begun. I became a hall chaplain of sorts. The guys would bring their non-Christian friends to me and say stuff like, "Yo, Steve, you better tell Anton he goin' to hell..."

So I told Anton he was going to hell, and Anton received Jesus. And the momentum continued. Over the course of that year, Jody and I saw almost a dozen of those guys give their lives to Christ. We personally discipled several of them. In the South, we'd call this a gullywashing, toad-strangling revival. You can call it whatever you want, but by any definition, it was a move of God. I even ran into one of those hell-raisers at a youth crusade I was speaking at a couple of years later. I asked him what he was doing there. He told me he was a youth pastor.

Do Something. Anything.

God poured out his Spirit and did something remarkable on our hall that year. The experience will probably keep its place as one of my top-ten audacious faith memories for many years to come. But the transformation didn't start with a sermon. Or a Bible study. Or dramatic signs and wonders. It started with ramen noodles and Dr Thunder. Because when you're in college, Dr Pepper and Mountain Dew might as well be Cristal and Dom Pérignon. So you settle for Mountain Lightning. And ramen noodles are your manna.

Sometimes audacity shimmers and shines. Most of the time the packaging is nondescript. I like to think God conceals his extraordinary intentions in ordinary people to protect the extraordinary value of his purpose in our lives.

Is there a need you can't stop thinking about that you're perfectly positioned to do something about? Do something about it. Anything.

Is there something you're good at that God could transform into greatness if you energized your efforts and focused your abilities for God's glory? Go for it. All the way.

Are there subtle tweaks you can make in your everyday interactions and activities that will give God some room to move in a miraculous way? Make room and get ready.

Of course, none of this is automatic. God's invitation for you to step out in audacious faith isn't going to fall from the sky and hit you in the head. You've got to train your eyes to look for it. The impossible becomes possible for you only as you carefully observe and faithfully obey the direction of the Holy Spirit. Yes, God wants to increase your influence and multiply your impact in more ways than you could ever imagine. But he doesn't always do that by calling you to make dramatic changes in your life overnight. He probably won't call your family to relocate to a remote jungle before the end of the month and translate the Bible into Braille for a tribe of blind cannibals. More likely, some ordinary opportunity or responsibility in your everyday life will seem to catch fire. Faith opens your eyes to see the potential to serve a God who is already at work on your behalf.

So don't leave all the good parts for the Christian-celebrity A list. Don't be disillusioned by a lack of special effects in your life. You're probably standing next to a burning bush right where you live and work. That's where audacity started for me. That's where audacity started for Moses. And it's a not a bad starting place for you.

CHAPTER 6

Wave Jumper

My five-year-old and I have a great time playing Wave Jumper at the beach during the summer. Here's a brief description of this Furtick family game.

I spend quite a while convincing Elijah that playing in the shallow part of the ocean isn't as fun as going out a little deeper. He looks uncertain. I insist. He hesitates but finally agrees. We start wading.

The whole time, I stand behind Elijah, he holds his arms high above his head, and I hold tightly to his hands. The farther he's willing to wade, the better. I take him out to the place where the water hits his chest. Then we wait for a big wave. When we see one rolling toward us, Elijah says he wants to go back to the shallow part. I convince him everything's cool. He seems relatively assured—enough to give this a try. "But just one time," he says.

Finally the wave arrives. Elijah screams to make sure I'm in position. I assure him that I'm right behind him. And at the last possible moment, just before the water wipes him out, I jerk him up. High enough that the ocean water doesn't spray his face or fill his ears—he hates getting water in his ears.

Elijah laughs uncontrollably. Then he proudly screams at the top of his lungs, "I'm the wave jumper! Let's jump another wave, Daddy!"

And we jump another one and another one and another one. What five-year-olds lack in strength they more than make up for in endurance. So much for "just one time."

I don't have the heart or feel the need to explain to my boy that, technically, he's not the wave jumper. Daddy is the wave jumper. He should probably scream something like, "I'm the hand holder!" We all know that Daddy is the one doing the heavy lifting here. In actuality, my son's assignment on Team Furtick is simple and minimal: to keep his hands reaching upward and trust that when the wave comes I'll lift him high above it.

This is the essence of audacious faith. In chapter 3, I referred to it as *sanctified naiveté*. It's also a picture of how our faith and God's faithfulness work together when we trust him to do great things. I know Wave Jumper isn't likely to catch on as a national pastime. But I think it illustrates one of the most common patterns in Scripture: As the big waves roll toward us, God promises to do the heavy lifting. He only requires that we have the faith to wade in as deep as he leads and keep reaching up to him.

Up to Here in Fear

When the people of Israel finally escaped Egypt, God led them through the desert toward an impassable barrier—the Red Sea. And there, with Pharaoh's army closing in behind them, they were trapped. What could God's people do? If they stayed on shore, they'd be murdered. If they forged into the depths, they'd surely drown. No wonder the Bible says they milled around in confusion, crying out in terror.

Then Moses announced the next move:

The LORD will fight for you; you need only to be still.
(Exodus 14:14)

"You need only to be still"? Now, I don't take this to be a literal instruction. Obviously God didn't mean for his people to physically stand still and wait for him to intervene. If they refused to move, Pharaoh's chariots would certainly run them over. Or maybe drag them back to the inhumane circumstances they had come from. So doing nothing doesn't seem to make much sense, considering that God had guaranteed his children safe passage into a land of promise and potential. Was this really God's Plan A? Moses must have meant something different. Maybe God introduced an alternate route at the intersection of fear and faith.

Take another look at Moses' surprising instructions. I see his words as equal parts promise and perspective.

Promise: "The LORD will fight for you."

Perspective: "You need only to be still."

Translation: It may be *your* job to cross over, but it's *God's* job to see you through.

If you'll do the believing, he'll do the achieving. And God did. Before their eyes, he parted the waters of the sea, and the Israelites crossed over in safety. (The Egyptian soldiers weren't so lucky.)

I hate to break this to you, because it might deflate your self-esteem. But technically, you're not the wave jumper. Yes, the risks of walking in faith are real. No, it's not a game. But remember, you're not alone in this by a long shot. Not only are you not alone, but you're also not even primarily responsible for the outcome of your obedience. Your heavenly Father has a firm grip on you. His vantage point is way above the water level. He's bigger than you. He's stronger than you. And he's got you safely in his grip.

It gets even better: When you get down to it, you're not the one holding on to him—he's holding on to you. Maybe you're afraid that if you pray a Sun Stand Still prayer and live by audacious faith, you'll end up letting God down. But the reality is, you were never holding him up.

He's the Wave Jumper.

Perhaps some very real fears are crashing in on you as you read this. Terrifying opposition may be breathing down your neck. What should you do?

Before you swim out any farther, be sure that God is the One leading you out into deep waters. Count the cost. Consider the ramifications. Apply wisdom. Then, once it's clear he is calling you into the waves, don't you dare let the magnitude of your fears send you back to dry land. Keep moving out deeper. Keep reaching up.

You'd better believe the classic scene on the shores of the Red Sea flashed before Joshua's eyes on the day he stared down the sun. How could he forget it? Ahead, water to the horizon. Behind, the dust clouds of Pharaoh's approaching army. And then the moment came: the Lord created a highway in an ocean and drowned the fighting forces of the most powerful nation in the world. Surely this image of God's faithfulness was burned into Joshua's spiritual retina.

If you're going to ask God for the impossible, this kind of perspective has to become a part of your permanent vision too. It will become a magnifying glass to bring your personal Page 23 purpose into focus. It will enlarge your heart as you pray Sun Stand Still prayers. The perspective of faith will lift you high above your fears, whatever they may be.

A lot of times, our greatest fears are rooted in personal insecurities. The perspective of faith enables us to see who we truly are in Christ. God is on our side. Through Jesus, we are righteous. We are cleansed. We're accepted.

If your greatest fear stems from a lack of resources to do God's will, the perspective of faith will show you the sufficiency of Christ. He is able to meet all your needs—not according to your supply, but according to his glorious riches (Philippians 4:19).

Maybe your greatest fear is the negative opinions of others. The perspective of faith won't totally silence that fear. It will just gradually make what God says to you more important than what others think about you.

If you're afraid of some of the gigantic changes you sense God is trying to make in your life, you need to know that your fear is normal. Not only are your fears normal, they're also valid. And they can even serve an important purpose. If you didn't have major fears about the big things God is calling you to do, I'd be worried. The goal of faith isn't to take away your fears but to leverage those fears to create bolder belief. Faith leads you past your fears and reassures you of God's presence. And after a while, you begin to trust that God is going to lift you above the waves *this* time just like he did *last* time.

I don't want you to live life as a would-be wave jumper like so many Christians who never wade into deep waters for fear of stingrays, shark attacks, and undertow. The One who creates, commands, and calms the waves is also able to keep you from going under.

At the same time, don't get overconfident in your *own* abilities to do something great for God. You'll end up thrashing around in self-reliance rather than clinging to God in faith. You've got to be careful. Otherwise you'll mistake arrogance for audacity. A healthy dose of fear can bring you to a place of dependence on Jesus. That's always a good thing.

CONFIDENT HUMILITY

Obviously, praying audacious prayers and walking in bold faith takes confidence. But healthy confidence is born out of genuine humility. The two must work in tandem. Confidence without humility is arrogance. Humility without confidence is weakness. Confidence and humility are both biblical. And they're equally essential for a life of true faith.

One day a leading military official approached Jesus. One of his most valuable servants was sick, and the outcome looked bleak. Jesus offered to abort his scheduled ministry activities and make a house call to heal the servant, but the commander offered an alternative. Study his response in Matthew 8:8. It's a textbook lesson in audacious faith bolstered by confident humility:

✶ "Lord, I do not deserve to have you come under my roof." *Humility.*

✶ "But just say the word, and my servant will be healed." *Confidence.*

Complete confidence in the competency of Christ matched with sincere humility. This is the only formula for authentic audacious faith.

Apathy refuses to take the chance. Arrogance sweeps you away to a place outside God's protective parameters. Either way, you'll miss out on the action if you aren't willing to get in over your head. Grab on to God with all you've got. Have faith that he can lift you high above your circumstances and fears.

I've noticed that he usually doesn't do it until the wave is just about to wash over us. That's what makes it faith. And that's half the fun.

THE PERHAPS PARADOX

It's encouraging to encounter another Old Testament character who overcame his fears and chose audacity in the middle of serious uncertainty. In 1 Samuel 13–14, we read that the army of King Saul had been locked in on the losing side of a standoff against the Philistines. Apparently Saul's troops spent most of their time looking for better caves to hide in (13:6). Eventually Jonathan, the king's son, became so irritated with the fear and inaction of his fellow warriors that he decided to make a bold move. He enlisted his armor bearer to join him on a two-man commando raid.

His battle plan was potentially God inspired—and a little ludicrous. The two young men would openly approach the enemy outpost. If they got a go-ahead sign from God, they would attack. Outnumbered. Outmanned. Underresourced. A borderline suicide mission. But if God was with them, Jonathan figured, nothing could stop them. All he had to do was persuade his bodyguard. Here's an excerpt from his motivational speech:

> Come, let's go over to the outpost of those uncircumcised fellows. Perhaps the LORD will act in our behalf. Nothing can hinder the LORD from saving, whether by many or by few. (14:6)

Wasn't Jonathan sending the ultimate mixed message? If you were trying to convince me to join you in an initiative this dangerous, I'd want you to do better than *"Perhaps* the LORD will act on our behalf." Perhaps? *Perhaps?* Jonathan seemed to be speaking out of both sides of his mouth. In one breath he communicated two opposing positions:

✴ "Nothing can hinder the LORD."

✴ "Perhaps the LORD will act."

At first glance, this seems like spiritual schizophrenia.

But *perhaps* Jonathan wasn't schizophrenic. *Perhaps* true faith always feels this way. On the one hand, I *know* that God is able to do anything. On the other hand, I *think* he's willing to do this specific thing. I know God can. And I'm pretty sure that he will. But I can't be completely sure.

That's where audacious faith comes in.

Audacity isn't the absence of uncertainty and ambiguity.

Audacity is believing that God's promise is bigger than my *perhaps.*

55 PERCENT SURE

Sometimes I stand up in front of my church, share a logic-defying vision, and wrap it with a bodacious assertion: "I *know* I've heard from God about this." Maybe I should be more precise. When I say that, what I mean is, "I'm as sure as I can be right now that I've heard from God about this." But I'm never completely sure. The only people who are completely sure they've heard from God are either clinically insane or under the influence of hallucinogens.

On a good day, I'm 55 percent sure. And that's enough certainty to take the next step.

The Bible says that God's Word is a lamp to our feet (Psalm 119:105), not a floodlight beaming to our destination. So, armed with the confidence that there's a *decent chance* and an *interesting possibility* that my impulse *might* be from God (*perhaps,* in other words), I start investigating.

And then the voices in my head start clamoring:

* *Who are you to claim you're hearing from God? You haven't had a decent devotional time in days.*
* *What if this fails? Lots of people are depending on you. The higher you set the expectations of those around you, the greater the possibility you'll let them down. Play it safe and stay put.*
* *Like you need another thing to worry about, oversee, or feel ultimately responsible for.*
* *Blah...blah...blah...*

Do you hear these same voices? Or am I alone in my schizophrenia? Both realities are valid:

* Hearing from God is exhilarating. His voice resounds with the possibility of progress. His instruction contains the seed of success, of change, of hope.
* Hearing from God is terrifying. If he wrote his will in the sky with fire, and airlifted you through the clouds to the completion of your assignment, obedience would be natural. But then faith wouldn't be necessary, would it?

We'd all like to live in a world where God lets us do big things that require minimal risk. Where the voice of the Holy Spirit carries for miles and miles, piercing through static and fuzz, jeers and taunts. If you ever discover that parallel universe, send me the turn-by-turn directions. I'll come and be your next-door neighbor.

The fact is, though, that the land where the sun stands still is a land where promises and perhaps must coexist. Audacious faith does not eliminate doubt and fear. It eclipses their power one decision at a time.

Let me give you a little insight into how this plays out for me as a pastor. I realize you may not totally relate to my experiences. Your situation probably looks a lot different. But I think you'll identify with the kind of tension I have to work through.

A lot of times, I feel fairly sure that God has placed a vision in my heart. But when it comes to believing that it's *really* going to happen, I start speaking out of both sides of my mouth. My wife, Holly, would verify this—and would probably provide a few more examples that I have conveniently forgotten.

Here's an example I remember clearly. I used to stand up in front of the core team that started our church and spew vision like a madman. I'd tell them about the thousands of people in our city who were far from God and how we were perfectly positioned to reach them. I'd paint a portrait of thousands of people worshiping Jesus united under the vision of our church. It was a challenging portrait to paint, since every Sunday night I was looking at mostly the same people who had been there the week before. And the week before that. On really good nights, we had more than two first-time guests. I think our first-time-guest welcoming team outnumbered our first-time guests roughly twenty to one.

One of the highlights of our early meetings was the night our children's ministry doubled in size. We declared it our children's ministry pentecost. A veritable revival. We had to call in the emergency children's ministry backup team to accommodate the tidal wave of supernatural blessing. Later I learned that one couple with five kids showed up, resulting in a net gain of 100 percent. That didn't stop me from telling the team, "We're growing. The groundswell has begun. We're gonna take this city!"

Then I'd go home and my perhaps would come smashing down like a sledgehammer. I'd ask Holly whether I'd made a mistake in moving to a big city when I was really just a small-town kid at heart. She'd say no, and I'd ask how she knew. She'd say she just did. That wasn't good enough for me.

"How do you just know?"

She'd remind me that God had made me a promise, surrounded me with a good team, given me a powerful vision, and gifted me in unique ways. And we could do this. We would do this.

I believed her. God is able. This is going to work.

Perhaps.

I'd stand up the next week and cast a vision for what seemed impossible. In front of the whole audience. Even if it was the same audience. And the next week I'd do it again. And again. And again. And I resolved to keep doing it until God's promise started to outgrow my perhaps. Eventually it did. But there were times when the fear almost wiped me out in the process.

When you reflect on God's vision for your life, you should be overwhelmed. You're going to wrestle with a lot of the same fears I experienced when I was trying to start a church in a new city. They're the same fears Jonathan and his bodyguard felt as they dared to charge the enemy hill, with one sword between them and no official military support. The same fears Moses, Joshua, and all of Israel felt while waiting for God to dry up the waters and drown the opposition. They're the same feelings my son Elijah feels when I'm trying to convince him to stop splashing around in two inches of foam and get out where the action is.

It's not wrong to feel fear. It *is* wrong to let that fear have the last word in your life. The people who accomplish the most astounding things for God's glory aren't the people who feel the least fear. Often they're the ones who deal with the most intense fear. But instead of letting that fear disable their dreams, they start increasing their capacity for faith. They act on the part of God's direction they *do* understand. And they leave the rest up to him.

SOMEONE HAS TO MAKE THE FIRST MOVE

Please don't wait until you have 100 percent certainty to follow Jesus boldly. Whatever you do, don't take your cues from the complacent Christians around you. Lots of people in your life might be perfectly content with kiddie-pool Christianity. But perhaps God is calling you to lead the way so that others can see a different example of the true nature of faith—an example that will fill them with a longing to experience his power. And someone has to make the first move. It might as well be you.

Jonathan and his armor bearer ended up saving the day in a spectacular way. They killed over twenty Philistines in that first attack. Their act of audacious faith was like an axis tilt that shifted the fate of an entire nation. In fact, when Saul and his six hundred leaders heard about the success of Jonathan's ambush, they came out of hiding. They attacked the enemy in full force. And God gave them a great victory.

I believe he's perfectly capable of doing the same for you.

What is your perhaps? What wave is God calling you to jump?

Is it a relational change? a financial leap? a costly sacrifice? a ministry opportunity? a drastic transition?

Remember this: God doesn't just show you which wave he wants you to jump next. He also positions his strong arm underneath to sustain you every step of the way. He knows every fear you're facing. He knows all the uncertainties you're navigating— only they're not uncertainties to him. Your perhaps isn't a perhaps from his perspective. To him, it's more like an opportunity for faith formation. And it's not just *your* faith he's building. If you'll go out deeper, he will use you to set people free all around you.

Be honest about your perhaps—with God and with others. Acknowledge, assess, and deal appropriately with your fears. Approach your impossibilities with confident humility. Pray that God will give you assurance of his presence and clarity in every decision you make. Through faith in his promises, keep yourself tightly connected to him. Be assured that he's got you in his grip.

And when the wave of fear or doubt crashes in…jump.

CHAPTER 7

Tiny Babies, Giant Faith

Wade and Ferris Joye are staff members at Elevation Church and two of the most godly people I know. They're also two of the most laid-back people you could ever meet. So when Wade came up to me one day bursting with excitement, looking as giddy as a schoolgirl, I knew there could only be one explanation: Ferris was pregnant with their first child. Or children, as it turned out. We found out later that Ferris was pregnant with twin girls.

The entire Elevation crew was excited. The men all started giving Wade manly advice. The women all started buying Ferris girlie necessities.

Then, out of nowhere, things got scary.

The day that your child is born is supposed to be a day of joy. For the Joyes, June 18, 2008, was a time of both joy and gut-wrenching uncertainty as their twin girls were born three months premature. Liana was born weighing one pound, fourteen ounces, and Adleigh was two pounds, five ounces. Each girl fit in the palm of Wade's hand. From the start, their chances of survival weren't good, and even if they did survive infancy, they faced a dire prognosis.

Things took a turn for the worse three days after they were born. Liana had a grade-four brain bleed that was the most severe the doctors had ever seen. It was so bad that they offered to take her off life support. The doctor told the Joyes that there was no way she would ever be normal. She might spend her life as a vegetable and never get out of diapers.

"When we heard the news," Wade recalls, "my wife and I hurried back to our hospital room and burst into tears. It felt like our world was crashing down around us. Everything seemed so hopeless. But we got right up from the bed and decided that we were going to fight for our girls. And we began praying our Sun Stand Still prayer. We boldly asked God that our girls would be healed and come home as healthy babies."

The Joyes urged the doctors to do everything possible for the girls from a medical perspective as they trusted God to do what only he could do. In the weeks that followed, the girls endured five surgeries between them, including a shunt placement for Liana and an intestinal surgery for Adleigh. And in addition to that, there were numerous infections and blood transfusions as well as countless other complications. Liana's lungs were in very bad shape until a last-resort treatment turned things around. There were times when one or both girls stopped breathing or their heart rates dipped dangerously low. Their parents watched and prayed as the nurses did what they had to do to resuscitate Ferris and Wade's precious daughters.

"It was an emotional roller coaster," says Wade. "Yet through it all, Ferris and I were determined to speak words of faith to our doctors, believing that our girls would defy the odds. When we felt scared, frustrated, and overwhelmed, we would post Scripture on their isolettes to remind us of God's promises. We asked for specific prayers on our blog, and it was truly amazing to watch how the church came together and prayed our Sun Stand Still prayer with us."

Since Wade oversees the worship ministry of our church, our leadership team decided to donate all the money made on the day we released Elevation's new worship CD in order to take care of the Joyes financially during this time. On the day of the CD release, I asked Wade and Ferris to share their story, and the church rallied around them and bought CDs like crazy. The Joyes got over eighteen thousand dollars to pay for the extra medical expenses and the many other needs they had during that time. We closed the service by singing a song Wade had written that helped him keep his eyes on Jesus while he was fighting for his girls' lives. The song was titled, rather appropriately, "Sun Stand Still."

Three months after their girls were born, Wade and Ferris's Sun Stand Still prayer was answered when Adleigh and Liana came home from the hospital. They were healthy and miraculously free from most of the issues that premature babies deal with. The doctors and nurses repeatedly commented on how amazed they were at the girls' progress. In fact, Liana is now walking and doing all the other things her parents had been told she would never do.

"I still think of how many of the experts told us that our situation was essentially hopeless," Wade says. "But we knew our God was bigger than that. He had spoken to our hearts and given us the faith to pray our Sun Stand Still prayer. We held on to that prayer no matter what setbacks we received, and God answered in a way that gave him all the glory.

"You will never know what it is like to experience God's power in this way until you have the audacity to *believe* and *pray* and *act* in the confidence that our God *is* a God of the impossible."

CHAPTER 8

The Surcharge of Sacrifice

I'll admit that what I'm talking about in this book sounds a little *out there.* I'm describing a kind of faith that lets you see invisible dreams and do impossible things. These are outrageous promises:

✴ You don't have to settle for the mundane. You can participate in the miraculous.

✴ God has a mind-blowing plan for your life. And even your everyday activities can take on exceptional meaning and have a massive impact.

✴ You seize these phenomenal opportunities by getting a personal Page 23 vision, praying your own Sun Stand Still prayers, and acting on your audacious faith.

How does all of this strike you? Overly simplified? Formulaic? Unrealistic? Too good to be true? Fairy tale–ish? Infomercial-esque?

If so, I understand. In a world of magic diet pills and no-money-down loans, you have every right to be skeptical about the claims I'm making. In fact, if you're not a little skeptical, you probably don't really understand the kind of faith I'm calling you into. Frankly, if you don't find yourself thinking, *Yeah, but what about...?* in response to some of the things I'm saying, I doubt you truly grasp what I'm trying to convey. After all, this way of life is counterintuitive and countercultural. It's borderline crazy.

So in this chapter—and throughout the rest of the book, really—I'm going answer some of your "Yeah, but what about...?" questions. Obviously, I won't get to all of them. Partially because I don't know the answers to some of them myself. But also because I don't want this book to take on the tone of a legal defense. I'm not out to bulletproof your belief system. I'm out to activate your faith and inspire your imagination.

Still, our thinking needs to be grounded.

Sun Stand Still prayers are miraculous, but they're not magical. You don't get to participate in a high calling without paying a high cost. A high calling for your life is God's gift to you. It's not something you earn. It's the product of grace. But unless you unpack your dream and put it to use, it's like an unopened gift. Effecting change in the world is rarely accidental. It's a result of intention and focus. You can't expect your miracles to come falling down out of the sky. The great things God will do through you are going to grow in the soil of persistence, prayer, obedience, and sacrifice. That means there will be plenty of plowing and pruning. That's the way living things grow, whether you're talking about vegetables or vision.

You will pay a tremendous price to operate in an audacious anointing. And the level of your impact will be directly proportional to the price you are willing to pay. Here's one way to look at it: faith is included in the contract of salvation, but activating your faith to realize God's vision for your life involves a surcharge of sacrifice.

Let me say it more directly. This deal is going to cost you. Significantly. When you ask God to do the impossible, he usually instructs you to do something uncomfortable. And inconvenient.

Salvation is free. Obedience can be very costly. These two facts aren't contradictory. In fact, this tension is at the heart of the gospel. How did God choose to accomplish the redemption of the world? By his grace—and through the willingness of Jesus to sacrifice his life. How will God accomplish the impossible vision he has planted in your heart? By his grace—and through your willingness to sacrifice your life for the sake of Jesus.

I'm not suggesting that you've got to work really, really hard for God to work in you. That's heresy. Grace is something *God* works *in* you. And by that grace, he works faith *out* of you.

But when you really understand God's work in you, your natural desire will be to surrender your life to him. To obey him unconditionally. That posture of surrender will result in radical steps of faith—and a confidence that flows from a heart that's fully devoted to God's plans. And in that place, past the edge of your comfort and convenience, God can raise your life to new heights.

Before we dare to ask God to do the impossible in our lives, we have to consider the cost that Christ has already paid. Then, in light of that ultimate sacrifice, we embrace the same mind-set. No sacrifice is too great for the sake of God's calling—and for the sake of the gospel.

The more worthwhile the reward, the more nerve-racking the risks. And before God can do an impossible work in your world, you need to let him do a deep work in your heart.

CROSSING OVER AND CUTTING AWAY

Just before Joshua marched around Jericho, an event took place that I don't remember ever hearing about in Sunday school. Maybe because it was centered around the subject of circumcision. My Sunday school teacher, Mrs. Gwen, probably didn't have the stomach for it. I don't blame her. To be honest, I'm kind of uncomfortable writing about it here. But it's just too important to skip over because it reveals a vital dimension of Joshua's trust in God and sheds new light on the price Joshua paid to lead such a powerful movement.

Most of the stories in the book of Joshua are war stories. Action adventures. So the big theme of Joshua's life—and the main focus of this book—is walking by faith. But occasionally God changes things up and introduces a twist in the plot. Like this one.

Just after the nation of Israel crossed over the Jordan River, God gave the Israelites a difficult assignment. Now that they were on the other side of the river, apparently he wanted to teach his people about a whole different kind of faith before they attempted to defeat their first enemy. Joshua 5 records the first thing God commanded Joshua to do before the launch of the most important conquest in the entire Bible. Brace yourself. This is painful and a little awkward.

> At that time the LORD said to Joshua, "Make flint knives and circumcise the Israelites again." So Joshua made flint knives and circumcised the Israelites at Gibeath Haaraloth. (verses 2–3)

Joshua made flint knives and did what? Yep. He did *that*. I'm sure you're familiar with the basics. Male circumcision isn't a big deal in modern times, of course. We've got hospitals. We've got medical technology. We've got educated doctors. And praise God, we've got anesthesia.

Plus, nowadays circumcision is usually performed on babies. This is definitely the most convenient time to do it. But these males who were being circumcised weren't babies. They were grown men. They didn't have access to Swedish steel surgical instruments. And they didn't have surgeons—or anesthetic. Ouch.

If you're new to the Old Testament, you've got to be wondering what this is all about. It must make God seem pretty sadistic. But the original audience who read the book of Joshua would have had a different perspective. To the Hebrew people, male circumcision was a physical sign of a spiritual covenant between the people and God. It was one of the most important elements of Jewish law. And it was an extremely meaningful event signifying God's promise to his people as well as their commitment to his commands.

In the New Testament, the same ritual takes place on a different level. God is more interested in our internal, spiritual condition. So the apostle Paul talks about a "circumcision of the heart," one that isn't merely "outward and physical" (Romans 2:28–29). This circumcision involves God cutting away everything in our lives that doesn't bring glory to him. Stripping away our pride and self-reliance. Teaching us to trust in him alone.

Honestly, I'm not sure which is more painful, Old Testament circumcision or New Testament circumcision. They both have the potential to be grueling. They both point to one timeless truth: God has to work *in* us before he can work *through* us.

With that context in mind, let's take another look at the Joshua story. You know by now that the generation who served under Moses lost the opportunity to cross over into the land of their inheritance. Despite all the evidence, they simply refused to believe that God was able to do the impossible. God wanted to bless them in ways that would have blown their ever-loving minds. But they missed out because they weren't willing to move forward in faith.

Joshua's generation was poised to do what the previous generation had failed to do. God was about to launch them into the experience of a lifetime. And they were not backing down. They were charging ahead, full of faith. But they hadn't been circumcised yet. And before God let them experience the fullness of his promise, he insisted on performing a painful operation.

What if they refused to endure the pain? What if they rebelled against the instruction? They could have written it off as a waste of time. They could have stood around slapping each other on the bottom, drinking bubbly, perfecting their "We just crossed over the Jordan River and we're so awesome" touchdown dance in the end zone.

But it's clear from the context of Joshua 5 that God wasn't going to allow the Israelites to move forward and occupy the land until they had obeyed his command to be circumcised. It was a Do Not Pass Go kind of deal. Good thing they chose to go under the knife. Otherwise, they wouldn't have been able to settle in the land.

At this point in the Sun Stand Still experience, you're probably at the same point in your journey. You've already crossed over a lot of old paradigms into a new way of thinking about God and a fresh vision for your life. And I believe that the generation we're living in is a Joshua generation. We're living in a time that Peter, James, John, and Joshua could have only dreamed about. Technology has presented us with more opportunities to advance the gospel and grow in our faith than any previous generation on the planet. There's never been a more exciting time to be alive. Unlimited impact is at our fingertips. Anything is possible.

But before we can claim the territory for God that he has promised us, our hearts will have to be circumcised. We have to go under the knife. We have to choose to take some costly steps of obedience to really follow Christ in audacious faith.

There's a lesson to be learned from the unbelief of Moses' generation: if you refuse to take God at his word and don't find the faith to cross over, you'll miss out on seeing him do the impossible in your life.

The lesson from the circumcision of Joshua's generation is equally important but a little more subtle: until you humble yourself and submit your heart to God's process of renewal, you can't go forward into the next victory he has planned for your life.

TRADE OFF TO TRADE UP

You may feel like this is a tangent that has nothing to do with the original reason you picked up this book. After all, we've been talking about God's ability to accomplish the impossible. Now we're talking about…circumcision?

Trust me. This isn't some sort of bizarre, superspiritual, touchy-feely sideshow. I want to deal with some of the subjects that are directly connected to your personal vision and audacious faith. They may even be the most crucial components. Not only do you need to believe in God's ability to bring you across the Jordan, but you also need to trust him enough to let him develop a heart of sacrifice and surrender inside you. It's tempting to want to skip right to the sun-stopping, river-crossing stuff—the increased influence, answered prayers, and electrifying experiences of God's presence. But that stuff won't be genuine and certainly can't be sustained if it isn't cultivated out of a heart that has been formed by the Spirit of God.

There's always a trade-off. Before God can bring his promises to pass in your life, he has to strip away all the stuff that keeps you from trusting him wholeheartedly. And that stuff is on the inside. God's invisible work in you prepares you for his visible works through you.

Certain components of spiritual success are easy to see. These are the tangible, public, and obvious victories that inspire you to admire well-loved heroes. But the training ground for those victories is the stuff you *can't* see. Crossing over into God's promise is always accompanied by a cutting-away process. And once you've crossed over the Jordan by embracing your Page 23 vision, there are some intense internal challenges waiting for you on the other side.

I don't know exactly what this cutting-away process will look like for you. God has a *personalized* calling for your life, so the sacrifices he calls you to make will be specific and unique. All sorts of variables play into this. The things that God will call you to lay down or walk away from will depend a lot on where you've come from and where he's taking you. And only he knows that. But since I've seen this scenario play out in thousands of lives (mine included), I can hypothesize about a few possibilities.

God may to have to cut away some of your self-centered dreams to make room for his bigger and better dreams. Maybe the desires of your heart are wrapped in ambition for status instead of passion for Jesus.

God has scheduled me for open-heart surgery on many occasions to deal with my distorted priorities and superficial motives. At times he's graciously allowed me to get my heart right by inspiring me to humble myself through fasting, prayer, and repentance. But other times, he chooses to strip away the ego and pride in my life through more drastic measures.

The thing is, sometimes God has to let your dream die so that his vision for you can come alive. I've met many great men and women of God who pinpoint the most confusing and agonizing failures of their lives as the impetus behind their most significant spiritual advancement.

A Divine Downsize

I know one businessman—I'll call him Kasey—who is absolutely certain *God fired him* from his job a few years ago. I wasn't aware that God worked in the HR department, but that's exactly how Kasey explained it to me. When he tells the story now, he does it with a smile. But at the time, he wasn't happy about it. In fact, for the first three months after he lost his job, Kasey was so bitter that he quit praying and going to church altogether.

His frustration was definitely valid. He hadn't done anything wrong. He had been working for a huge power company, doing a good job, and moving up the ladder fast. In a span of just seven years, he had gone from making minimum wage to pulling in a salary larger than anything his dad ever dreamed about making. And at the rate he was going, Kasey thought he might retire by age forty-five.

Unfortunately, at the rate he was going, he was also going to lose his family and potentially shipwreck his faith. His wife was tired of having him home for dinner fewer than three nights a month. As much as he tried to make up for his absence by adding more square feet to the house and filling it with overpriced furniture, his wife didn't really want another couch in a new room. What she wanted was for him to watch a movie with the family on the couch they already owned. She didn't tell him until years later, but she already had a plan in place to leave him if something didn't change.

But God stepped in and initiated a divine downsize. The way it happened seemed unfair. Kasey's boss asked him to lie to another supervisor about the violation of a safety regulation. However, Kasey was an honest Christian man, so he challenged his boss. His boss pushed back, but Kasey refused to budge. So the supervisor went into the records, forged some phony low ratings on Kasey's old performance reviews, and showed him the door.

For eight months he suffered the reality of unemployment. He was depressed and demoralized. Then he remembered a message he'd heard at our church about how God often has to cut away our selfish goals to make room for the gospel in our lives. Kasey then realized that, before he was let go, he had been praying a Sun Stand Still prayer that God would use the platform of his success to make him a witness for Christ. Now the question loomed: was he willing to follow Jesus into a place of costly obedience?

What if God wanted to answer Kasey's Sun Stand Still prayer by giving him the courage to act with integrity, even if the result was a loss? What if the impossible thing God wanted to do in his life wasn't tied to another raise but rooted in a decision to forgive people who acted unethically and deceitfully? What if God decided to bless my friend with more bandwidth to focus on his marriage and children instead of another bonus check to pad his portfolio?

God used this season of setback to strengthen Kasey's faith— and keep the most important things in his life intact. At first he didn't understand why a loving God would take away the things that mattered most to him. Now he realizes that when God removes something from our lives, it's not because he's trying to take away something good. It's because he's trying to make room for something better. For my friend, that something better was a strong, God-glorifying marriage and a chance to recalibrate his calling. In fact, Kasey has since moved to another state to head up the missions department at a growing, vibrant church. During the next year alone, he'll have the opportunity to send more than a thousand believers overseas to dig wells and care for orphans.

None of this would have happened if God hadn't fired my friend. Do you see it? The same divine downsize that threatened to break him down laid the foundation for God to build him up to a greater height of peace and potential.

You and I must count the cost of our calling. Will we let God take away something we want now in order to make room for the thing we ultimately want?

You're reading this book because you ultimately want to be connected to God's plans and purposes. You ultimately want the abundant life Jesus died for to course through your veins and flow from your life. And to get to that stuff—the best stuff—God may need to cut away a lot of other junk.

It's a trade-off. It will definitely cost you something. But it's always a trade-up. Why? Because God always gives back so much more than he takes away. When God takes something or some-one out of your life, he's just clearing space on your hard drive for an upgrade. Hebrews 12:11 sums it up well:

> No discipline seems pleasant at the time, but painful. Later on, however, it produces a harvest of righteousness and peace for those who have been trained by it.

DIVINE VISION CREATES DIVISION

I can't think of a more vivid and comprehensive biblical example of someone who paid a high price for a big dream than the story of Joseph. God gave Joseph a personal and controversial vision of influence before he turned eighteen. That teenage vision be-came the engine of Joseph's entire existence. It lifted him to heights of unimaginable opportunity. But it also stripped him of everything he knew and separated him from everyone he loved. Before God positioned Joseph to save an entire nation, he cut away all of Joseph's security and tested all his loyalties.

Talk about audacious: Joseph calls a family meeting one day, skips the small talk, and drops the news. "Just so you know, I'm taking over. One day, you'll all bow down to me." And in case anyone is prone to argue with his assessment, he throws down the God card, explaining that this play call came directly from heaven.

Joseph's bold vision turns his family against him. Instead of embracing Joseph's destiny, his older brothers opt to beat him half to death. Then they sell him into slavery in Egypt. Years later Joseph's obedience results in a whirlwind of false accusations, wrongful imprisonment, and worst of all, deep isolation and betrayal. His vision doesn't fully come to pass until thirteen years of loneliness and pain have come and gone.

Yet the Scripture insists that the Lord was with him through it all. And eventually Joseph rose to become second in command of Egypt and to play a redemptive role in Israel's future. (You can read Joseph's dramatic story in Genesis 37–47.)

It's hard to understand how the Lord could possibly be with someone who is going through such a dark time and paying such a high price. Unless you choose to believe that God wasn't passively standing by, watching his servant suffer. Apparently, God was using every setback Joseph suffered to set up his life for great spiritual significance.

I think Joseph sensed that. I think it's what kept him hanging on. What else did he have to hold on to? His sense of calling helped him maintain certainty and clarity no matter the adversity. Even when it meant he had to stand all alone.

At some point your audacious vision will get you beat down. And sold out. And left alone. Hopefully not to the extent of Joseph's experience. Few of us will ever taste physical abuse and solitary confinement for the cause of Christ. But often the hardest pain to treat is the type we can't see, originating in places we can't reach, resulting in symptoms we can't completely describe.

I've seen wives embrace an audacious vision to bring their marriages under the lordship of Christ. But it was almost impossible for them not to second-guess God's voice when their husbands initially became more resistant, rather than running to the altar to repent. What was that about? What were the wives supposed to do next?

When I was sixteen and began to share my life's vision with my friends, very few of them set aside a percentage of their income to give an offering to my future ministry efforts. Very few of them even gave me the obligatory, "We'll pray for you about that!" (I should note here that I had a few wonderfully support-ive friends, lest they read this and become *former* friends. There just weren't many.) Instead of volunteering support, many of my peers effectively disinvited me from the cool-kid parties. Some of them said they wanted "the old Steven back." That was the one thing I couldn't give them. Because when you get a vision from God, it burns your old paradigms to the ground. In a way, I think they were trying to put me back in my place. Complacency isn't very comfortable in the presence of audacity. I'm glad I stayed put, looked ahead, and kept dreaming.

Whether your vision is met with cheers or jeers, outside opin-ion cannot be your sustenance. Man cannot live by bread alone, and he certainly can't survive on a steady diet of attaboys. He who lives by the approval of others will die by the absence of the same.

Don't let anybody but God himself put you in your place. And don't stop forging ahead when you encounter opposition. The fact that you're fighting big battles means that you're close to even bigger blessings. The reason you're facing fierce resistance now is that God is preparing an astonishing reward in your future.

THE SIGN OF YOUR SURRENDER

Is God cutting away an area of your life right now—a motive, a dream, a relationship, or some other source of false security deep within you? If so, take it as a sign that something better is soon to come. Paul said that "our present sufferings are not worth com-paring with the glory that will be revealed in us" (Romans 8:18).

A high calling often exacts a high price. But it always yields an astronomical return. When God comes toward you with the flint knife, remember that he's not out to hurt you. He's aligning your desires with his desires so that he can accomplish the impossible in your life. And once you've made up your mind to pay the price and to trust the Lord with all your heart, no level of spiritual achievement is out of reach. Because when you want what God wants for the reasons he wants it, you're unstoppable.

Are you ready to make the commitment your calling requires? If so, I invite you to declare this pledge with me:

By God's grace, no matter what it costs me, I'm going to live by audacious faith. I'm going to believe God for the impossible, to accomplish by and for him what I cannot accomplish on my own. No matter what people think about my Page 23 vision for my life, I'm going to take God at his word. I'm going to trust him with my whole heart and follow him step by step, even when my surrender requires sacrifice. Even if it seems like he's taking me over the edge, I will trust that he'll be there to catch me if I fall. I will trust that he is good and that somehow, someday, he will work all things in my life together for my good and his glory.

CHAPTER 9

The Simplest Systematic Theology Ever

I hope you're getting it by now—your vision should never be limited to *who you are* or *what you think you can do*. Let's face it: apart from Christ, we're completely incapable of doing anything of eternal value. Most Christians agree on that point.

But here's where it gets a little trickier: the size of our vision isn't even determined by *who God is*. If it were, we'd all be curing AIDS and eliminating global poverty, and everyone on the planet would have heard the gospel at least seventeen times.

Instead, the scope and impact of your vision will be determined by *who you believe God is*—and whether you have the courage to respond accordingly. If you're going to have a Page 23 vision and pray Sun Stand Still prayers, you've got to have the right idea about who God is *to you* and what he wants to do *through you*.

When I was in college, I came across a paradigm-shattering concept in a book called *The Knowledge of the Holy* by a twentieth-century writer named A. W. Tozer: "What comes into our minds when we think about God is the most important thing about us.... Were we able to extract from any man a complete answer to the question, 'What comes into your mind when you think about God?' we might predict with certainty the spiritual future of that man."

A lot of very smart people have referenced that quote over the years, and with good reason. If Tozer is right, this single belief—our belief about who God is—defines every component of our Christian lives. It's the starting point for almost every spiritual decision we will ever make.

Our view of God is the most important thing about us.

In this book, we're exploring what happens when you dare to believe God for the impossible. Defining your Page 23 vision brings a major part of that picture into focus: What is the impossible thing God wants to do *through* you? *for* you? *in* you? How should you specifically apply the message of audacious faith today to your life? your family? your finances? your business? your ministry? your broken relationships? your unmet desires? From one angle, this thing is all about *you*. Through examining your passions, your pain, and your priorities, you're answering a timeless question. It's the same question Jesus asked a blind man named Bartimaeus one day: "What do you want [God] to do for you?" (Mark 10:51). How do you need him to strengthen you in this specific season of your life? to empower you to make a difference in your world? The impossible vision God wants to accomplish in your life is tailored *just for you*. This isn't a book about Joshua's historic faith or someone else's impossible dream. This message is all about you—right here, right now.

Yet at the same time, the impossible vision God wants to accomplish through you has absolutely nothing to do with you. It's all about *him*. Audacious faith is more than an attitude. It's much more than simply believing in yourself and what you are capable of. True faith is founded on what you believe about God and what he is capable of. The key to unlocking your audacity is not to take the most bizarre risk you can think of, then blame the outcome on God. The key is getting a clear and correct view of God, believing that God is actually who he says he is. And that he can do what he says he can do.

Yes, you have to determine your vision—exactly *what* impossible thing you're asking *for*. But you can do that only if you know *who* you're asking the impossible *of*.

So two seemingly contradictory realities are both true. Faith has *everything* to do with you. And it has *nothing* to do with you.

Welcome to the conundrum of audacious faith.

I could write story after story about men and women who asked God for the impossible. I could cite endless Bible examples of people who dared to believe they were created and saved to do more than settle for the lowest common denominator of faith. The book of Hebrews says that these were people "who through faith conquered kingdoms, administered justice, and gained what was promised; who shut the mouths of lions, quenched the fury of the flames, and escaped the edge of the sword; whose weakness was turned to strength; and who became powerful in battle and routed foreign armies" (11:33–34).

But until you have the right, biblical picture of God, this is all just a history lesson. Without an accurate vision of God, you cut yourself off from the very One who enables you to have audacious faith in the first place. You see, great men and women of faith don't have some special spiritual DNA that God injected into them. What makes them unique actually has very little to do with them. Because when you get down to it, they are no differ-ent from you and me: full of fear, plagued by sin, and riddled with insecurity. What makes world-changing Christians unique, au-dacious, and powerful isn't their perfection. It's their understand-ing of God's perfect nature and purposes in the world. *This* God is someone worth taking risks for. *This* God is someone worth praying Sun Stand Still prayers to. What these men and women of faith believe and experience firsthand about God drives them to settle for nothing less than extraordinary faith. And in the same way, what you believe about God will directly determine the legacy of your faith and your impact on the world for the glory of God.

Of course, you and I can't ever completely understand all the mysteries of God. Good thing we don't have to. Those men and women of faith didn't either. I'm sure of it. The only One who has mastered the nature of God is…God. Great people of faith simply get a grip on a handful of essential truths—and then they hold on to those truths for dear life as they follow Christ in faith, one step at a time.

In this chapter, I want to nail down what it truly means to have faith in God. Don't panic. This isn't a systematic theology book. I'm not going to delve into divisive, confusing, or abstract theories here. I just want to front-load your faith with an under-standing of the two most important truths you need to know about God. An understanding of these two facts alone will be more than enough to enable you to ask him to do the impossible.

See? I'm making this as simple as I can. I'm looking out for you. A theology lesson based on only *two* points. What else would you expect from a guy who squeezed a three-year seminary edu-cation into five and a half years? (I was never a very good student.) One of the theology books I was assigned during my illustrious career clocked in at over twelve hundred pages. I was bleary-eyed and brain-dead by the end of that one. Don't get me wrong. I appreciate the extensive and comprehensive research that goes into a book like that. And I love learning new things about God. I really do. But after pulling a few consecutive caffeine-filled all-nighters to get through it before the end of the semester, I emerged with a simplified perspective. Everything I really need to know about God I learned in the prayer we prayed at the dinner table when I was a little kid: "God is great, God is good, and we thank him for our food."

Ignore the food part. And overlook the way *good* and *food* don't really quite rhyme. Once you get past that, this prayer is actually a remarkably elegant summary of the character of God. Two things you need to know about him:

God is great.

God is good.

There you go. The theological training that cost me tens of thousands of dollars…condensed into the first sentence of a children's prayer.

Is it really that simple? I believe it is. I'm not saying that's all there is to God. But I would say that everything we'll ever need to know about God is simply an extrapolation of one of these basic characteristics: God's greatness and God's goodness.

I'm sure you're not very impressed by my profundity or originality here. Maybe you were expecting something a little deeper. I understand. After all, we're attempting to comprehend the vast and incalculable nature of God. It's natural to want to hang your theology on something a little more solid and substantial. But I am convinced that most of what we need to know about God is stuff we already understand. We simply haven't begun walking in the light of what we know to be true. I call that action step *activating your audacious faith*. The minute you take one step, and then another, into these truths, your life will change. By God's power, you'll break through into the kind of life you were created to live.

To be fair, this minicatechism didn't actually begin as a children's prayer. It's straight out of the Scriptures:

> One thing God has spoken,
>   two things have I heard:
> that you, O God, are strong,
>   and that you, O Lord, are loving.
>   (Psalm 62:11–12)

What's the psalmist saying? God is strong. He's *great*. And God is loving. He's *good*. These two truths are the only solid foundation for real trust in God. There's no better place to start building your audacious faith than on the greatness of God.

GOD IS GREAT

This book invites you to believe that you were made to experience the miraculous on a regular basis. And if you are going to take impossible risks for God, you had better know that he has the resources to get his will accomplished on earth.

If he is not able to make the sun stand still, why waste your breath asking him to do so? Faith in a God who is not able to deliver on what he has promised is not audacious. It's absurd. If I were in financial trouble, I wouldn't go to a college student to bail me out. I'd approach someone with a balance sheet that was more robust than mine. Anything else would be a waste of time.

The thing is, no prayer of faith to a great God is a waste of time. The measure of God's abilities will always surpass the measure of our audacity. No prayer is too big for our God. No vision too sweeping. No risk too great. God has never been nervous about his ability to live up to our faith in him. This amazing fact invites us to believe him for the kind of requests and goals that most people would consider outside the realm of possibility.

If there is no limit to what God can do, then there is also no limit to what we can dream or pray or accomplish in his service.

Our God spoke the universe into existence. Then he stooped down and measured it with his hand (Isaiah 40:12). Did you know that scientists have found stars that are as large in circumference as the entire *orbit* of Jupiter? Yet God did not spend a single ounce of energy in creating them. He simply said, "Let them be." And they were.

Our God is the One who leveled Jericho's walls while Joshua and the children of Israel walked laps in childlike obedience.

Our God is the One who took on flesh and walked among us, opened blind eyes, and raised dead people to life. And remember, not only did he walk on water—he enabled an ordinary fisherman to walk on water with him.

The God of the Bible can do whatever he pleases. And what pleases him is to show off his power for his glory and renown. So give him the opportunity. Dream God-worthy dreams. Pray faith-fueled prayers. Live a life that can be explained only by the existence of a God who is infinitely great.

STRONG ENOUGH TO DO THAT

Elijah came to me recently when I was working out (or "extra-sizing," as he calls it) and told me he wanted me to bring his pirate ship downstairs. It's a pretty big ship—way too big for a five-year-old to carry—so he was reduced to begging me to do the job for him. From his limited perspective, absolutely nothing was more important in that moment than the safe and immediate transportation of this toy pirate ship. To me, the need wasn't quite so urgent. I tried to blow him off. He tried to wear me down. I didn't budge. Neither did he. Finally he tried a different angle: "Daddy, I really need my pirate ship. Do you think you're strong enough to do that for me?"

Smart kid. When all else fails, appeal to Daddy's pride. Elijah got his pirate ship, and I got a lesson about how God sees the needs of his children. He likes to show off his strength and display his power. But he doesn't do it to protect his pride. It's all about demonstrating his glory.

If your problem is too big for you, it's just the right size for God. He's strong enough to do that for you, whatever your *that* may be. Why would you strain to do all the heavy lifting when you have a God like this as your Father?

> The LORD your God is God of gods and Lord of lords, the great
> God, mighty and awesome. (Deuteronomy 10:17)

> Who is this King of glory?
>   The LORD strong and mighty,
>   the LORD mighty in battle. (Psalm 24:8)

Their Redeemer is strong;
   the LORD Almighty is his name. (Jeremiah 50:34)

The God we serve is able to save us. (Daniel 3:17)

When we see God for who he is, our small dreams are eclipsed by his unlimited strength as it becomes increasingly clear that there is nothing our Father in heaven cannot do.

GOD IS GOOD

Psalm 62:11 isn't complete without the counterpart concept in verse 12.

You, O God, are strong,
   and...you, O Lord, are loving.

The two sides of the coin are inseparable: God is strong *and* he's loving. He's great *and* he's good.

It's one thing to acknowledge that God is great. Most major world religions recognize that much about their respective deities. What sets the Christian faith apart is an unrelenting hope in the fact that God is good. That fact was settled once and for all on the cross. And it's really good news. After all, what good is infinite power if you have no access to it? Yes, God does whatever he desires. Thankfully, what he desires is to make his power and resources available to you. Then he wants them to seep from every pore of your life.

God's goodness means that all his greatness is meant to work in your life *for your good*. Not necessarily your momentary happiness. But your ultimate good. Romans 8:28 says, "We know that in *all* things *God works* for the *good* of those who love him, who have been called according to his purpose." That isn't a statement of probability. It's a revelation of the unchanging character of God. "Good" describes what God has been, is, and will always be doing.

The survival of your audacity depends on your knowing deep down that your God is good. Knowing God is great enables you to dream, pray, and live beyond your means because you know he *is able* to respond. That's half the equation. But knowing God is also good enables you to dream, pray, and live beyond your means because you know he *wants* to respond. Until you believe God is with you and for you, fear and hesitation will characterize your life. While you may believe God is capable of accomplishing the impossible in and through you, you will not necessarily believe he *desires* to work through you. The result will be faith paralysis.

Here's another reason you've got to learn to cling to the goodness of God: Sometimes the pressure of your daily struggles can push your belief system beneath the surface. Immediate pain and struggle can color the lens through which we view all of God's past, present, and future activities in our lives. We can easily lose track of the truth. And in that kind of emotional haze, it doesn't take long for us to start thinking that the goodness of God is a lie.

But look back over your life. Remember. No matter what you've been through or what you're going through now, God has been good to you. You're here. You're alive. You're breathing. He has let you see another day. And he has brought you to this page with a sincere desire that you will experience more of him.

He has been good to you.

And when you remember that fact, it changes the way you see your challenges. David said it like this:

Praise the LORD, O my soul,
and forget not all his benefits—
who forgives all your sins
and heals all your diseases,
who redeems your life from the pit
and crowns you with love and compassion. (Psalm 103:2–4)

David could have focused on his failures. Instead, he remembered and focused on God's forgiveness. He could have focused on his diseases. Instead, he remembered and focused on how good God had been to heal them. He could have focused on the pain of the pit. Instead, he remembered and focused on the fact that God had pulled him out of it.

Difficulties are going to come. Walking with God sometimes means walking through trials. But instead of focusing on your situation, remember God's goodness. Let it permeate your thoughts and emotions. Because whatever your past performance or present struggle, God is with you to help, save, and heal.

He will, because he is a good God.

And remember this: He has been better to you and me than we deserve. We're saved, forgiven, and redeemed by the power of God. And even if he never does anything else for us, his single act of love on the cross demonstrated his goodness for all time. You might be going through such a fiery trial in your life right now that you've lost sight of the supreme expression of the grace of God. Remember the cross. Jesus was mocked, spit upon, and beaten beyond recognition so that we could become righteous. He became the scum of the earth for us, carrying the weight of all our sins so that we could know forgiveness and enjoy eternity in his presence. In that place of suffering and death, God settled once and for all the truth that makes audacious faith not only possible but also irresistible. And nothing you and I could do or say or believe or suffer will ever change it.

God is good. Always has been. Always will be.

"DON'T LOOK AT ME, MAN…"

I was always a small kid growing up. Small kids usually get picked on a lot, but I was a bit of an exception. I was small, but I also had a crazy side to me. When you're trying to pick a winner in a fight between two kids, a good rule of thumb is to go with the one who is crazier, not necessarily the one who is bigger. However, one day I accidentally bumped into a bully at my middle school whose size no amount of craziness could conquer. You know the kid I'm talking about? The nineteen-year-old eighth grader who can't seem to make it out of middle school and who served time in prison during elementary school? This guy was over seven feet tall, and I swear he had a mustache. Maybe I'm exaggerating—a little. But you get the idea: the dude was pretty fierce.

Accidentally bumping into this bully—we'll call him Skull-Crushing Giant—turned out to be one of the worst mistakes of my life up to that point. You see, Skull-Crushing Giant—or SCG—interpreted my clumsiness as a sign that I wanted to fight him, when in fact nothing could have been further from the truth. I was truly clumsy.

Nevertheless, I'd bumped him, he'd been slightly inconvenienced, and only one option occurred to his small, brutal mind: revenge. Only one option occurred to me too: run as fast as my short, white legs could carry me.

Now, since SCG was over nine feet tall (he's growing, I know), it wasn't long before he caught up with me. But it had been raining outside, causing SCG's shoes to become slippery. Therefore, just as he reached for me, he slipped. And fell. Some people laughed. But SCG didn't think it was funny. And I didn't think it was funny when SCG got up off the ground, grabbed me by the collar of my shirt, and jacked me up against the wall.

From my vantage point high against the wall, I could see a crowd starting to gather to witness the execution. I scanned the crowd, looking for friends or family. Luckily, I saw one of my best buddies. Big heart. Super nice guy. And I could see he was trying to mouth a message to me. But exactly what was he was trying to communicate?

Don't worry—I've got your back, man.

No, it wasn't that. He was saying something else. What? I squinted in his direction, desperate for hope.

He tried again. His lips were moving, but I noticed his body wasn't coming in my direction. In fact, he seemed to be backing away. Strange.

Finally he gave up on mouthing the message. He shouted at the top of his voice, "Don't look at me, man! I can't help you!"

Oh, thanks…Judas.

Um…somebody else, help?

Now let's pause for a moment and examine the characters in this junior-high tragedy. Maybe we'll find God somewhere in this story.

I think lot of people would identify my friend as the God

FALSE BELIEF ABOUT GOD

figure: He's got good intentions but limited strength. A super nice guy, no doubt. But powerless to help...or even try. Millions of Christians view God as a warm-hearted, caring, and comforting buddy. But, although they'd never say it this way, deep down they believe that he's too feeble, too distant, or too overwhelmed by evil to do anything about the pain and suffering in the world he created. In fact, when a crisis breaks out in your life, or on a global scale, maybe you subconsciously picture God as standing by, watching helplessly, backing away, saying, "Don't look at me, man."

How could you possibly put your faith in a God like that? If God has good intentions toward us, but no power, then his goodness does us no good. He is unable to come to our aid when we need him. He feels for us, but he can do nothing for us. It's impossible to trust a God like that to do the impossible in your life.

On the other hand, I was in the death grip of Skull-Crushing Giant. He had plenty of power—and the worst possible intentions. Unfortunately, this is the image of God that has been created in the psyches of many believers. And you certainly can't trust the bully version of God any more than you can trust the scared-buddy God. If God had all the power but only bad intentions, then we would have every reason to be terrified of him. He is infinitely powerful, so if his intentions toward us aren't good, we should all fear for our lives. We should stay out of his way. And if we should ever, God forbid, bump into him, we should run for our lives. Not only is it unthinkable to ask a God like this to do impossible things in our lives; it's also unwise to ask him to do anything at all. The best strategy is to avoid him completely. Which is, sadly, the route many people wind up choosing.

Do you now see why the image that comes to your mind ✗ when you think of God is the most important thing about you? You can't believe for impossible things from a God you find it impossible to believe in. And I don't mean *believe* in the technical sense of the term. I'm talking about grounded, anchored, immovable trust. Audacious faith. The kind that receives God's vision and acts on his promises, the kind that is based on his unflawed character and unchanging nature.

So, I know you're on the edge of your seat, wondering, *Whatever happened to that skinny kid pinned against the wall?* Fortunately for me, in the moments just before my death, a savior appeared. Her name was Mrs. Dupree. She was the most feared teacher at Berkeley Middle School. She had the power. She wasn't afraid to use it. And everyone knew it. She also happened to be a good teacher, and she sort of liked me—at least enough to spare my life. So she had good intentions. And the minute Mrs. Dupree entered the scene, SCG knew he was outgunned. He had met his match. He calmly returned me to my normal, upright position and walked away. I thought about yelling at him, "Yeah, you'd better walk away." But I didn't. I also thought about kissing Mrs. Dupree. I didn't.

I hope you're rejoicing as I relive this happy ending. More importantly, I hope you're seeing a picture of the God you serve. He's like Mrs. Dupree, only a whole lot bigger and a whole lot better. He is infinitely powerful, but his intentions toward you are infinitely good. He is capable, but he is also compassionate. He not only has created a good plan for you, but he is also able to bring it to completion in your life.

Build your confidence in his goodness and his greatness, and he will do the impossible. In our day. In your life. For his glory.

CHAPTER 10

Hear. Speak. Do.

I'm not content to just motivate you to *want* to live with audacious faith. I want to enable you to develop your faith. It's one
thing to *want* to trust God to do impossible things through your
life. It's another thing to get to a place where you're *able* to trust
him at that level.

No one can transplant a heart of faith into you like it's a new
body part. Faith is more like a muscle you already have. It just needs
to be strengthened. You have to be intentional about making it grow.

I'm not saying that you're on your own with this thing or that
you have to work up some feeling of faith through your own ef-
fort. You're *not* out there by yourself. There are millions of Christians across the world exercising audacious faith right alongside
you. And of course, there's the divine presence and power of the
Holy Spirit inside you.

But what I want to talk about in this chapter is even more
basic. I want to go back to the source document of our faith: the
Bible. See, the Bible is no mere book. It's a living document. You
might say it's a living *force*. We call it the Word of God because in
it God spoke—and still speaks.

In a way, the living Word is what audacious faith is all about. Praying a Sun Stand Still prayer might take you to all sorts of new places, but it will never take you one step away from the Word of God.

The Bible describes a process of faith formation, one that integrally involves the Word at every step:

* Hearing the Word *initiates* faith.
* Speaking the Word *activates* faith.
* Doing the Word *demonstrates* faith.

3 POINTS FOR MESSAGE

Let's break these down one at a time.

HEARING THE WORD INITIATES FAITH

Romans 10:17 says, "Faith comes from hearing the message, and the message is heard through the word of Christ."

There's only one place you can acquire faith: you've got to go to the Word of God. And in the pages of the Scriptures, as God's promises become personal to you, your faith potential is ignited. Hopefully that's what's been happening to you as you've been reading. Each biblical example of audacious faith should cause your own spiritual circuit board to light up. The same thing happens every time you go to church and hear a sermon from the Bible.

So to live by audacious faith, you're going to need to become very familiar with your Bible. You're going to need to saturate your mind with the Word of God. If your faith isn't rooted in God's promises, it's not scriptural faith. It's just wishful thinking.

Remember, Joshua had the right to pray a Sun Stand Still prayer because his prayer was based on a promise God had made to the Israelites. God had promised to fight for them. God had promised to defeat their enemies. Joshua was occupying the Promised Land that God had guaranteed to his people. So Joshua's confidence didn't spring out of a void. It was born out of God's Word, which had been integrated into Joshua's thinking and shaped the way Joshua saw the world.

You can't claim God's promises if you don't know God's promises. That's why God specifically commanded Joshua:

> Be strong and very courageous. Be careful to obey all the law my servant Moses gave you; do not turn from it to the right or to the left, that you may be successful wherever you go. (Joshua 1:7)

In order to be successful, Joshua had to be obedient. And obedience comes only by hearing and doing the Word of God. Hearing comes before doing.

To really pray with power and to trust Jesus radically, you need to consume as much of God's Word as you possibly can. Increase your exposure to teaching and preaching about Jesus. Prioritize the presence of God in your daily life. That's where the power of belief takes hold and the process of true faith begins.

SPEAKING THE WORD ACTIVATES FAITH

This is one of those things that I didn't learn growing up in church. And honestly, the first time I heard about speaking God's Word, the whole concept seemed kooky to me. It conjured up images of monks singing Gregorian chants and televangelists preaching fiery sermons at 2:00 a.m.

But over the last several years, God has shown me how important it is to speak his Word in my daily life. It's sort of a missing link for a lot of Christians. A lot of people get *information* from the Word of God, but no real *transformation* happens as a result.

So if hearing God's Word is like turning the key in the ignition, then speaking God's Word is like putting the car in drive.

Every time you encounter God's Word, the potential for faith is born. And this isn't just a one-time thing. It doesn't just apply to saving faith—the type of faith that initially brings you into a relationship with God. This is also the way faith is introduced into every single area of your life. When you hear the Word of God concerning a particular issue, need, or reality, the possibility to increase your faith is in play.

But then it is your responsibility to activate that faith. And you do that through *speaking* God's Word. Let's review the details of God's instructions to Joshua again:

> Do not let this Book of the Law depart from your mouth;
> meditate on it day and night. (Joshua 1:8)

I think most of us subconsciously translate that command to mean: Do not let this Book of the Law depart from your *heart.* Or from your *mind.*

But that's not what God said. He specifically told Joshua to keep his Word in his *mouth.* Before Joshua could make his Sun Stand Still prayer, he had to make the ways and words of God a natural part of his vocabulary—in speaking to others and in speaking to himself.

Some of the best sermons I've ever preached in my life have not been delivered behind the pulpit at my church. Some of the best messages on faith I've spoken weren't written down for the world to read in a book. The best leadership challenges I've issued have not gone forth at conferences all across the nation. Some of the best sermons I've ever preached in my life have been the ones I've preached to myself.

In fact, I preach to myself all the time. I've preached sermons to myself that were so good I wanted to give myself an offering and respond to my own altar call. I *have* to preach to myself just to keep going sometimes.

Some days I get frustrated with my own inconsistency. I feel like I just keep letting God down over and over again. So I preach to myself from Lamentations 3:22–23:

> Because of the LORD's great love we are not consumed,
>   for his compassions never fail.
> They are new every morning;
>   great is your faithfulness.

And as I speak God's Word to myself, I'm reminded that God's mercy can convert the mistakes of my past into wisdom for my future. It's a new day.

Some days I feel weak and limited. The vision that God has put inside me seems so much bigger than the resources around me. So I preach to myself from 2 Corinthians 9:8:

> God is able to make all grace abound to you, so that in all
> things at all times, having all that you need, you will abound
> in every good work.

And as I rehearse this guarantee, my faith is reactivated. My perspective is renewed. I recalculate my resources according to what God's Word says instead of what my mind thinks or my emotions feel.

How many times during his leadership tenure do you think Joshua revisited God's words to him about being strong and courageous? I like to imagine that just before he laid it all on the line that day and commanded the sun to stand still, he muttered under his breath, "Be strong and courageous...be strong and courageous...be strong and courageous..."

And let me assure you, this speaking-the-Word thing isn't just for preachers like me and Bible heroes like Joshua. If you want to get really good at walking in audacious faith, you have to get really good at preaching God's Word to yourself too.

You see, there are going to be many points along the way when you're not going to have anyone around to motivate you or encourage you. And in those moments, you'd better be able to open God's Word, look in the mirror, and remind yourself of the truth. As you incorporate God's Word into your vocabulary, the way you see your circumstances will begin to shift. Your faith will start to rise higher than your feelings and your fears. And it all starts with speaking the Word.

I know you may not feel competent to preach to yourself. Maybe you don't know enough Scripture verses to even get started. I'm going to help you with that by giving you my concise compilation of the biblical principles that are most applicable to your daily life. My Twelve Audacious Faith Confessions aren't actual Bible verses, but each one is based on the comprehensive teaching of God's Word. So whatever circumstances you're facing in your life right now, you can begin to preach God's Word to yourself—starting today.

Ready? Let's preach.

Twelve Audacious Faith Confessions

1. I am fully forgiven and free from all shame and condemnation.

> Romans 8:1–2; Ephesians 1:7–8; 1 John 1:9

2. I act in audacious faith to change the world in my generation.

> Joshua 10:12–14; John 14:12

3. I have no fear or anxiety; I trust in the Lord with all my heart.

> Proverbs 3:5–6; Philippians 4:6–7; 1 Peter 5:7

4. I am able to fulfill the calling God has placed on my life.

> Exodus 3:9–12; Psalm 57:2; Colossians 1:24–29

5. I am fully resourced to do everything God has called me to do.

> Deuteronomy 8:18; Luke 6:38; Philippians 4:13

6. I have no insecurity, because I see myself the way God sees me.

> Genesis 1:26–27; Psalm 139:13–16; Ephesians 5:25–27

7. I am a faithful spouse (if you're single, you can slip *future* in there) and a godly parent— our family is blessed.

> Deuteronomy 6:6–9; Ephesians 5:22–25; Colossians 3:18–19; 1 Peter 3:1–7

8. I am completely whole—physically, mentally, and emotionally.
   > Psalm 103:1–5; Matthew 8:16–17; 2 Corinthians 5:17;
   > 1 Peter 2:24

9. I am increasing in influence and favor for the kingdom of God.
   > Genesis 45:4–8; 1 Samuel 2:26; Acts 2:37–47

10. I am enabled to walk in the sacrificial love of Christ.
   > 2 Thessalonians 2:16–17; 1 John 3:16; 4:9–12

11. I have the wisdom of the Lord concerning every decision I make.
   > 2 Chronicles 1:7–12; Proverbs 2:6; Ecclesiastes 2:26; James 1:5

12. I am protected from all harm and evil in Jesus' name.
   > Genesis 50:20; Psalm 3:1–3; 2 Thessalonians 3:2–3

How much difference would it make in our lives if we would preach these realities to ourselves? Let's resolve now to preach God's Word in our own hearts daily, emphatically, convincingly!

YOU'RE HEREBY ORDAINED...

Immediately after I introduced these Faith Confessions to our church, inspiring stories started flooding in. I knew the concept of speaking God's Word would be fresh and compelling for most of our people. But I had no idea how powerfully God would use this simple exercise to explode wrong thinking and reorient self-images.

One woman whose husband had recently abandoned the family told me that reading these confessions and speaking God's Word with her children each night had given her the will to keep living. Since she started speaking God's Word daily, her friends and family say they can sense God's peace radiating from her life.

One teenager wrote to tell me about how she had been cutting herself in the bathroom at school because she felt ugly and unwanted. But she had started to renew her mind each day, several times a day, by speaking, "I have no insecurity, because I see myself the way God sees me." As she did so, the need to dull the edge of her self-loathing mind-set gradually subsided. Last I heard, it's been over six months since she cut herself.

A business owner asked if we could give him a stack of these confessions to pass on to everyone in his company. He said that in over thirty-five years of being a Christian he's never felt more closely connected to God's purpose in his work life than he has since he started speaking God's Word.

If it worked for them, it will work for you too. Speak the Word as your first expression in the morning. Speak the Word over your family and friends all through the day. Speak the Word to yourself each night as you process your failures and celebrate your victories.

This may be a new practice for you. It may feel weird the first couple of times you try it. You may have never preached a sermon before, and you don't feel qualified. That's okay. I hereby ordain you as a preacher of the gospel of Jesus Christ: to yourself. (This does not legally authorize you to conduct weddings and funerals—just thought I should clarify.)

DOING THE WORD DEMONSTRATES FAITH

Before we get too crazy preaching in the mirror, there's a sobering warning in the Bible that we need to look at. The book of James scathingly confronts people who claim to have faith but refuse to do something about it. James sums it up this way:

> Faith by itself, if it is not accompanied by action, is dead. (2:17)

So it's possible for us to *hear* God's Word, take notes, memorize Scripture, and speak God's Word out loud until everybody thinks we're smoking crack, yet never walk in true audacious faith. Because it's not really faith until we *do it. Authentic faith doesn't end in a positive mental state. It plays out in total obedience based on the sure Word of God.*

One time, Jesus told his disciples to get in a boat and head out to the next ministry appointment while he stayed behind to spend some time in prayer. The disciples dutifully complied. Jesus neglected to tell the disciples, however, that they would encounter a storm along the way that would threaten to end their lives. That's where things get interesting. We'll pick up the story in Matthew 14:25–29:

> During the fourth watch of the night Jesus went out to them, walking on the lake. When the disciples saw him walking on the lake, they were terrified. "It's a ghost," they said, and cried out in fear.
>
> But Jesus immediately said to them: "Take courage! It is I. Don't be afraid."

"Lord, if it's you," Peter replied, "tell me to come to you on the water."

"Come," he said.

Then Peter got down out of the boat, walked on the water and came toward Jesus.

In this single, simple biblical account, all three of the stages of faith formation I've been describing are on full display.

It starts with Peter *hearing* the words of Jesus. This is how his faith is initiated. It's what transforms him from just another terrified disciple in the boat to a potential water walker. He recognizes Jesus' voice. He realizes the potential of the moment. This is the man who could possibly save his life. But at this point, his faith isn't out in the open. It's just starting to rise inside.

As you read this book and digest God's Word, your level of belief is lifting. It's initiating your faith and expanding your horizons. But that's not the finish line—it's just the beginning. You're still in the boat. You've simply *heard* the Word.

The next step is to *speak* it. To activate the faith that has been initiated. Peter does this when he shouts back to Jesus, "If it's you, tell me to come." What's he doing? He is vocalizing an expression of his faith. He's committing verbally. He's taking it public. He's putting this miracle in motion.

But the deal isn't done at this point. We don't teach this story to our kids in Sunday school because Peter and Jesus carry on an interesting conversation. This story is memorable and fascinating because Peter *gets out of the boat* and transcends the law of buoyancy. It's not until his foot hits the water that his faith is demonstrated. It's not until he risks failure, embarrassment, and physical harm that the supernatural power of Jesus starts working on his behalf.

Your faith isn't going to magically increase simply because you want to do big things for God or because you'd like to be able to sleep better at night. Your faith can mature only as you methodically develop it through God's faith-formation process:

* Hear the Word.
* Speak the Word.
* Do the Word.

When you get into the rhythm, you'll notice your faith getting more muscular. Not all at once. It builds little by little with each step you take in faith. You'll notice your outlook getting clearer every time you bring the Word front and center in your decisions. You'll learn to let the Scriptures dominate emotions of discouragement and frustration. You'll feel the strength of the Word enable you to press on through resistance that would have stopped you in your tracks before.

And if you'll commit to a life of consistently hearing, speaking, and doing the Word, your faith will start to swell and your spirit will gain size incrementally but substantially. It might even grow strong enough to stop the sun or walk on water.

GOD'S WEALTH OVERFLOWS TO ME IN AVALANCHES OF ABUNDANCE.

CHAPTER 11

The Solid Ground of Audacious Faith

When you're trying to convince people to do something difficult, you usually go on and on about how capable *they* are. You assure them *they've* got what it takes. In essence, you want them to know you believe in them.

But audacious faith doesn't work that way. It's not based on who *you* are or what *you* can do. Audacious faith is based on who God is, what he's already done, and what he will continue to do.

In chapter 9, I laid down a simple two-part theology of audacity—God is strong, and God is good. In this brief chapter, I want to prepare you for how God will show these giant truths about himself to you over the course of your new life.

He will show himself faithful.

It is *he* who will prove that he's got what it takes. The unfailing faithfulness of God—not our capability or performance—is the solid ground of our journey in audacious faith.

God didn't encourage Joshua according to Joshua's faith. He

encouraged Joshua according to his own faithfulness. On the day Joshua was appointed leader over Israel, God said:

> No one will be able to stand up against you all the days of your life. As I was with Moses, so I will be with you; I will never leave you nor forsake you. (Joshua 1:5)

In other words, God based his argument on his own ability: "I'm with you. I won't leave you. That's your confidence. That's your hope."

Joshua's experience goes to the core of the gospel. In fact, when you study the Bible as a whole, you discover that the story of the Scriptures is a story of a faithless world being rescued and redeemed by a faithful God.

In the book of Genesis, it was a faithful God who didn't give up on faithless Adam and Eve even after they blatantly disobeyed him and rebelled against his commands.

Then it was a faithful God who found a man named Noah after the entire human race had turned away from him in faithlessness. And through the faith of this one man, God preserved the human race.

Then it was a faithful God who chose a man named Abraham and called him out of a place called Ur. He used Abraham to create a nation whose people were destined to be more numerous than the stars of the sky or the grains of sand on the seashore. Abraham wavered in his faith. But God never wavered in his faithfulness.

It was a faithful God who recruited a fearful man named Moses to bring his people out of cruel Egyptian bondage and slavery.

It was a faithful God who raised up a new leader named Joshua after the faithless generation who refused to enter the Promised Land died off in the wilderness. His people took territory and defeated enemies because God was fighting for them, even when they fought against God's purposes through their disobedience and unbelief.

It was a faithful God who raised up judges to deliver the people of Israel as they sinned against him and did what was right in their own eyes. But when they cried out to him for help, he heard them and faithfully delivered them.

It was a faithful God who selected an unlikely shepherd boy named David to shepherd Israel according to God's own heart. Nobody else was even considering David as a candidate for the kingship. But God raised him up to replace a faithless king named Saul and lead the nation into a time of unprecedented favor and blessing.

It was out of the lineage of King David that the faithful One, Jesus Christ, appeared on the scene to rescue his people from their sins. Faithfully, Jesus led the perfect life we could not live. Faithfully, he went to the cross and died the death we should have died. Faithfully, God raised him from the dead, defeated sin and death, and opened the way of life for all who will believe.

God's faithfulness continued throughout the time of the apostles as he sent his promised Holy Spirit. The Spirit set the church on fire, enabling them to baptize three thousand people on the Day of Pentecost. To cast out demons. To heal crippled people. To send out evangelists to tell the world the message of Jesus Christ.

And it has been a faithful God who has enabled lives to be changed through Jesus long after the last word of the New Testament was recorded. It has been God's faithfulness over the past two thousand years that has caused the gospel to spread to every continent, overcome all opposition, and convert billions of people who were once far from God.

God's faithfulness extends to your own life. It is a faithful God who has allowed you to breathe every breath you've ever breathed. It is his faithfulness that has enabled you to experience the highest mountaintops of your life. It is his faithfulness that has enabled you to endure the darkest valleys. His faithfulness is the reason for every victory and success you've ever experienced. His faithfulness is your hope in every defeat and failure.

So before you read another page, make this clear distinction in your heart: *My faith is in Jesus, the Son of God, the Savior of the world. My faith isn't even in my ability to believe in Jesus, because sometimes I won't be able to perceive him. Sometimes I won't be able to feel him. Sometimes I will have doubts. But my faith isn't in any of that. My faith is in his faithfulness.* Second Timothy 2:13 says,

> If we are faithless,
>> he will remain faithful,
>> for he cannot disown himself.

Our faith may fail. But God's faithfulness never will.

Remember, too, that God's faithfulness is not just about looking back. It also sets your destiny in forward motion. In fact, his past faithfulness is the best predictor of his future ability to make the sun stand still in your life. In the days and years ahead, you will face circumstances that seem insurmountable. Every brain cell inside your cranium will be tempted to doubt.

At those times, remember and rehearse: Our audacious faith is not built on the fault line of feelings or the flood plain of our performance. We build our faith on solid ground. Higher ground. We build on the faithfulness of God.

CHAPTER 12

Mistake into Miracle

When I first met Norm, I thought he was one of the nicest guys I'd ever met. But what I didn't know was that he was about as far from God as a person could get. I could tell he was carrying a lot of pain, though. And it was hard to miss him. He must have weighed in at over three hundred and fifty pounds. When Norm started coming to Elevation, we had only about fifty people in the room. Norm sat in the back every week, crying like a baby through the music, then hanging on every word I preached. Obviously he really wanted to be there. Even though he lived over an hour away, he always found a way to get to church.

Over the course of several months, we watched Norm open up his heart to God. It was amazing. He'd had very little exposure to Jesus during the fifty years of his life. He'd ignored God for so long that at first the concept of grace seemed too good to be true. But he eventually decided to take God's word for it and place his faith in Christ. We all celebrated. It took two of us to baptize big Norm in the swimming pool at the high school where we met on Sundays. People screamed and cheered and chanted his name. Norm wept and hugged me so tightly that I thought he might crush my spine. And in the next few months, everybody became a big Norm fan. He was easily one of the most beloved volunteers at Elevation Church.

Then one afternoon Norm requested a meeting in my office. I could tell it was urgent. When he arrived, he looked upset and nervous. He was shaking. His opening sentence went something like this: "I'd totally understand if you want to kick me out of the church after what I'm about to tell you."

I assured him that it would be tough to shock me—and then told him to fire away. So he opened fire. "Pastor," he said, "I think I'm going to prison soon."

Okay. That shocked me.

Turns out that Norm had been involved in some illegal online activity before he accepted Christ. He explained in detail what he had done, and he promised me that it was all in the past. Unfortunately, the charges were just now being brought, and the parties bringing the charges could care less that Norm had experienced a life-changing encounter with God. As far as they were concerned, he was a criminal. They were determined to do everything in their power to send him to prison for a long time.

After thirty minutes of pouring out his heart and telling me how sorry he was to embarrass the church like this, Norm paused and looked across the desk. "Is there still a place in this church for a guy like me?" he asked.

"Norm, we started this church for people like you," I told him. "We started this church for people who are far from God. If there wasn't a place for people like you in this church, I wouldn't want to be the pastor."

Of course he started to cry, because he's a big softie. We prayed together, and before he left, I promised him that not only would we not throw him out, but also we would do everything in our power to stand by him. And we did.

During his trial, our staff and volunteers rallied around Norm with prayer, counsel, and open acceptance. I brought him up on the stage one Sunday and shared his story with the whole church. I told them how Norm had confided in me that if it hadn't been for God's grace, he would have ended his life. But now, with the help of his church, he had the faith to stand. The church gave him a standing ovation. And, of course, Norm cried again.

Norm refused to lie about what he'd done, so he pleaded guilty to all the charges. At the sentencing, the judge dropped the hammer on him. Norm was sentenced to serve the full forty-eight months in a federal prison. When I heard the news, I was devastated. I asked Norm to come to my office right away, thinking I'd have to help him hold things together and lift his spirits from the depths of depression. But when he arrived, Norm's perspective shocked me. In fact, he was smiling.

"Pastor, you know I don't want to go to prison," he said. "Nobody does. I'm a little scared, like you'd expect. But I think God has some work for me to do there. So I don't want you to feel sorry for me. But I do have a favor to ask."

I told him I'd do anything I could.

"I need this church to train me," he said. "I need you to teach me how to tell people in the prison about Jesus. I want to go in there and make a difference for God. I want to take what I've experienced here at Elevation and start an Elevation in the prison. Will you teach me how to do that?"

So we taught Norm how to do it. And once he started serving his sentence, we began sending him transcripts of my sermons every week. Before long, he had started a Bible study, and since he didn't know how to prepare sermons, he just read my sermons to the guys. In the months since he went behind bars, several inmates have given their lives to Christ.

Norm has written us to tell us how God is starting a revival in his prison, halfway across the country. And how he's working out, losing weight, and getting buff. He says we won't recognize him when we see him. And he says we won't believe some of the stories he has to tell about how God has used him in that prison.

Norm isn't letting his past failures define his future.

Norm is believing there's a purpose in his prison sentence.

Norm has seen God turn his mistake into a miracle.

THE HARDEST KIND OF SETBACKS

Maybe you're beginning to think all this audacious faith stuff isn't for you. It's not that you don't *want* to live this way. You long to have a dream, pray impossible prayers, and take bold steps. But like Norm, you've messed up big somewhere along the way. You've wasted time, hurt people, and fallen short—maybe over and over again. And now you don't feel qualified.

This chapter is for you.

God wants to turn *your* mistake into a miracle too. You don't have to hand in your dreams and resign your faith. You can ask God to create a clean heart inside you and begin a new day all around you.

I've noticed that most of us don't have a hard time believing that God's grace is real—we just have a hard time believing that it's really available to *us*. We know all the reasons why God should pull us out of the game and bench us. All the junk from our yesterdays looms large in our minds when we try to think about what God wants to do through us today.

Each of us has our own personal catalog of screwups and failures. Maybe you did something incredibly stupid years ago and you're still paying for it. Maybe your mistakes are more recent. Maybe you have wasted some years that you know you'll never get back. Maybe you haven't honored your marriage, haven't finished your degree, haven't paid your bills, haven't been there for your kids...

Maybe you're in real trouble right now, and you know in your heart that you have no one to blame but yourself.

Those are the hardest kinds of setbacks to overcome—the ones we create for ourselves. It's natural to see the potential for redemption when someone else fails. But when we fail, it can feel like the game is over.

Let me assure you that if you have a little bit of faith left, it's not over. Many people would say God can still use you *despite* your failures. I want to take that a step further. God's grace is so audacious that he will use the *failure itself* to show off just how capable he is. In other words, I'm not just saying your mistakes don't disqualify you for a miracle. Your mistakes can actually make you a *more likely candidate* for a miracle—if you process them God's way.

Of course, if you take what I'm saying out of context, you could really abuse this principle. *Hey, since God wants to use my mistakes to show off how powerful he is, watch this! I'll make a total mess out of my life. Then God will have room to perform a really huge miracle.*

It doesn't work that way. We always reap what we sow. You and

I always suffer negative consequences from destructive choices. That's one of the reasons God has given us such specific commands about how to live. He knows what's best for us. And no true child of God should ever sin on purpose, presuming that God's grace will clean up the mess afterward. The fact that God can turn our mistakes into miracles isn't a permission slip to make more mistakes.

The apostle Paul directly addresses this in the book of Romans. After assuring his readers that there's no shortcoming God's grace can't cover, he addresses the obvious tension:

> Shall we go on sinning so that grace may increase? By no
> means! We died to sin; how can we live in it any longer?
> (Romans 6:1–2)

God's grace isn't a license to sin. It's not cheap perfume that we can splash on to cover up the stink of our failures. His grace is a priceless gift of mercy that invites you and me to move *by his strength* toward real wholeness in every area of our lives. Grace is the power to transform us through and through.

The first miracle of audacious faith isn't that God undoes all the damage that we've created over the years in one day. Instead, he miraculously begins a process of change inside us. That's where it starts. Because God can't turn our mistakes into miracles unless we first let him heal our hearts through biblical repentance.

REDEFINING REPENTANCE

I'm not sure what comes to mind when you think of repentance. Probably something along the lines of groveling, beating yourself up, and feeling really, really, really bad about what you've done wrong. And no doubt, the heart of repentance is humility. You can't truly repent if you aren't grieved by your sin in the light of God's holiness. You've got to face up to your wrongdoing before you can truly put it behind you.

Maybe you've never done that. That could be the first step toward turning your mistake into a miracle. Get honest about your failure. Assess the damage your sin has caused. Stop making excuses. Don't even try to play off the pain. Get it out in the open. If you've wronged someone, go to that person and seek forgiveness. If your sin is just between you and God, stop trying to hide it from him, and spend some serious time confessing your sin to him.

God can't make anything miraculous out of your mistake if you don't call it what it is and deal with it accordingly.

But that's only one dimension of repentance. After you've come clean before God and authentically owned up to your sin, don't wallow in it. And don't you dare try to make up for it. You can't. That's why Jesus died. That's the whole point of the gospel. God sent his Son to redeem your life because you could never redeem yourself. Believe that. Receive it. And then let God begin to replace the pain of your past with hope for a new future.

Yes, there's a time to bow down in repentance, but there's also a time to get up and move on. That brings me back to Joshua. (See Joshua 7–8.)

He was devastated after the army from a little town called Ai defeated his fighting men—and only days after the astonishing victory for Israel at Jericho. Ai was supposed to be an easy win. So Joshua had sent in his junior varsity troops to handle business. But unknown to Joshua, there was a dynamic playing out behind the scenes that was sabotaging his success.

When the Israelites had conquered Jericho, God had told them not to keep any of the plunder for themselves. They were to destroy *everything*—no exceptions. But an Israelite named Achan apparently thought the rules didn't apply to him. He had kept a little of the loot for himself, and the whole nation suffered for his disobedience. Because of Achan's rebellion, God had to show his people that when he tells them how they're supposed to do something, obedience isn't optional. So he allowed them to be routed by this unlikely group of people from Ai.

Since we have the benefit of knowing the whole story, we can see how the consequences at Ai were directly connected to sin in the Israelite camp. But Joshua didn't know all that yet. The only thing he knew was that he had led his people from the greatest victory in their history straight into a humiliating defeat. I'm sure he was filled with regret and self-doubt.

Whatever specific emotions Joshua was feeling, we know he was in a dark place, because the Bible says he tore his clothes and went into deep mourning. He blatantly questioned God's purpose and wondered whether he would ever recover from this setback. But God interrupted Joshua's downward spiral into self-pity and depression:

> The LORD said to Joshua, "Stand up! What are you doing down on your face?" (Joshua 7:10)

God responded to Joshua's desperate plea for help, but not in the way we might have expected. He didn't tell Joshua to beg a little more earnestly or perform an act of penance to prove he was really sorry. Instead, he told him to get up off the ground, stop crying about past defeats, and obey God completely in the present moment. Specifically, God singled out Achan in front of the whole nation and commanded that Achan and his family be put to death. Capital punishment for the whole family seems like a brutal and unfair punishment to our modern minds. But God was trying to keep his people free from the idolatry that could destroy them.

Sure enough, once they'd gotten rid of the sinful element among them, they marched into Ai (this time with the big guns) and blew their enemies away. God granted the Israelites a second chance, a decisive victory, and a valuable lesson on the subject of repentance.

THE BEGINNING OF A MIRACLE

Maybe you've spent the last several months—or even years—face-down on the ground, feeling defeated by foolish mistakes. It's possible you even thought your posture of guilt and remorse was equivalent to repentance. If so, I have a feeling God would say the same thing to you that he said to Joshua: "What are you doing down on your face? Stand up! Repent! And move on to your next victory."

In the book of Revelation, God hammers the church at Ephesus. He accuses them of losing their first love for Jesus. But I want you to notice something interesting about the way he tells them to remedy their situation. He instructs them:

Remember the height from which you have fallen! Repent
and do the things you did at first. (Revelation 2:5)

This verse helps me think about repentance in a brand-new light. God doesn't beat the Ephesians into submission through shame and guilt. Instead, he tells them to remember the height from which they had fallen—and to get back there right away. How? Through genuine, biblical repentance.

Technically, the New Testament term for repentance means to "change your mind." To align your thoughts with the thoughts of God. To get on his wavelength and embrace his plan.

But we see from Revelation that repentance also means to get back to the top. Back to God's perspective. His ways. His truth. His high calling and perfect plan for your life.

God wants to turn your mistake into a miracle. He wants to re-instate your faith and elevate your life to the old heights—and even higher ones. He did it for David after a terrible cycle of sin, denial, scandal, and depression. He did it for Peter on a lonely seashore following a flat-out betrayal. He did it for Joshua after a crushing loss to an inferior foe. He did it for my friend Norm in a federal penitentiary.

You have every reason to believe he's ready and able to do the same for you. You can have full confidence that, by the grace of God and through the power of genuine repentance, your mistakes don't have to be the end of God's vision for your life.

Suppose your life has been smashed to pieces because of sexual sin. It doesn't mean you're useless as an instrument in God's hands. In fact, if you're willing to let God mend and restore you, it could be just the opposite. There's a good chance God may use you one day to help put others' hearts back together when they find themselves in the same situation. Or better yet, maybe the pain you've experienced will sound the alarm and keep somebody you love from going down that same dark road in the future.

Or let's say you've squandered years of a certain friendship because, up until now, you've been too stubborn to forgive. What if God can enter that wrecked relationship and do something miraculous—*even now*? It won't be easy. You'll have to humble yourself, face the situation, do the right thing, and trust God with the part you can't control. But over time, maybe that relationship could become a trophy of God's reconciliation. Maybe this will be your opportunity to understand and demonstrate God's unconditional love in a brand-new way.

These are just a couple of common situations. I can't pinpoint every mistake that might be holding you down. It could be something so embarrassing that you'd be mortified to disclose it to anyone. On the other end of the spectrum, it may seem so insignificant that you've convinced yourself you can bury it and get back to business as usual.

Let me settle this once and for all: nothing you've ever done is so repulsive that God can't redeem your potential and love you through it. And the small stuff matters as well. The very sin you've been ignoring and minimizing may be the one that's limiting your ability to rise to greater heights in God. The most powerful sin in your life is the one you haven't confessed yet.

If you want to see God do the impossible in your life, you can't try an end run around the things you've done wrong. Don't hide them. Don't deny them. And certainly don't crumble beneath the weight of them. Bring them to Jesus. And let him make something miraculous out of them.

CHAPTER 13

When the Sun Goes Down

This is the chapter I wish I didn't have to write. But it may be the chapter you've been waiting for since the beginning of the book. A chapter that wrestles with the fact that even after you've asked God in faith for a miracle, it may not come.

Without acknowledging this obvious reality, the message of audacious faith will become incompatible with your life experience somewhere along the way. You'll eventually file this message away with all the other plans and promises you tried on for size that didn't work out. And we need to do everything we can to avoid that.

But I want to be careful. Because there's a good chance you'll misunderstand what I'm about to tell you. The goal of this chapter isn't to let you off the hook. If anything, I want to sink the hook deeper. I want to enable you to walk in audacious faith no matter what comes your way.

When we started this book, I made an audacious claim, and I've spent almost every page substantiating this assertion: *I have seen the sun stand still*. I stand by it. I've seen God answer prayers with miracles. I've seen people physically healed in a way that left doctors speechless. I've seen couples who had been infertile give birth to healthy boys and girls. I've seen people lose their jobs, pray, and quickly land new jobs that pay twice as much and require a fraction of the travel.

Sometimes—a lot of times—it goes that way. Faith works. Prayers produce. Praise God. There's nothing better.

But sometimes—a lot of times, honestly—it goes the other way. Sometimes the sun doesn't stand still. Sometimes the sun goes down.

Sometimes you pray your best, most honest, heartfelt prayers—and there is no answer. Or the answer is no. Sometimes, even though your motives are pure, your desire is good, and your need is urgent, the breakthrough doesn't come. The turnaround moment doesn't occur. The cancer spreads. The finances get tighter. The marriage feels more lonely. The kids grow more distant.

Sometimes the sun keeps sinking down, down, down...and no amount of hoping, fasting, or right living seems to stop it.

Remember, before Joshua ever saw the sun stand still, he had to watch in agony as the sun set slowly on an entire generation. Yes, God gave him the privilege of leading the charge into the Promised Land. But not before he was forced to endure forty years of wilderness wandering because of someone else's hesitancy. It wasn't his fault or his lack of faith. He believed. He wanted to obey. Joshua even did everything he could to persuade Moses to see the situation through eyes of faith. But that generation couldn't see through the doubts and dangers, so Joshua didn't get to inherit the promise for a long, long time. Joshua spent a large part of his life living in the shadow of a setback. And I imagine there were days when he wondered whether the sun would ever shine again.

Maybe you're living in a similar shadow right now. You thought you'd be a lot closer to completing your life goals by now. And you're pretty sure that you've done your part to make them happen. But someone else let you down. Something snuck up from behind and knocked you out cold. A crisis came along and crippled your ambition to do great things for God...or even expect anything good from him at all.

These seasons of setback can be fatal to your faith. It's easy to lose your way when the sun goes down. You can easily slip into a deep spiritual sleep in an attempt to escape the pain.

Or you can choose to convert your times of crisis into the greatest opportunities of your life. It all depends on how you see your crisis—and whether you seize the chance that lies before you.

I can't in good conscience promise that God will make the sun stand still every time you walk in audacious faith. Your faith does not control God—in fact, human faith on any scale can never put divine providence in your back pocket. Which means that sometimes people you love will get sick and they won't recover. You won't achieve everything you attempt. You'll have to absorb and manage some pain you didn't create, invite, or deserve. You'll have days filled with frustration and misery.

Audacious faith does not guarantee a crisis-free life. But audacious faith does enable you to seize the opportunity to see God's glory in the midst of every crisis in your life.

Even when—and maybe *especially* when—the sun goes down.

THE CRISIS CONUNDRUM

One night a while back, I was watching TV as a well-known public figure was addressing the current state of crisis in our country.

He rattled off examples of the stuff that's keeping many Americans up at night: home foreclosures, corporate downsizing, insurmountable debt—all the usual suspects. The picture he painted was bleak. I was starting to feel mildly depressed. But just as I was about to change the channel, the speaker flipped the script and delivered his punch line.

"The Chinese word for crisis," the man noted, his voice inflection picking up dramatically, "is a very interesting word. In fact, the Chinese word for crisis is made up of two distinctive characters that are very instructive for us in our current crisis. The two characters that make up the Chinese word for crisis are *danger* and *opportunity*. And so it is. Yes, these are times of great danger. Intense pressure. Unprecedented challenge. But these are also times of phenomenal *opportunity*. We must see past the danger and embrace the opportunity in our crisis."

I was inspired. And intrigued. I sat up in my bed, scrambled for my notebook, and started scribbling notes as fast as I could. Then I started brainstorming every possible biblical example of opportunities that God provided for his people. Old and New Testament. Familiar and obscure. Corporate and individual. And you know what I discovered? Every time God presents a significant opportunity, it's formed in the crucible of crisis. It's connected to danger. And it comes at a great cost.

Unfortunately, I later learned that the Chinese word for crisis doesn't necessarily mean "danger plus opportunity." It's an urban legend. So, technically, my man's motivational speech missed the mark.

But theologically speaking, the concept is right on. Most of the major opportunities recorded in the Bible were born in crisis. And the greatest opportunities in our lives come out of crisis too.

The glory of God often shines the brightest when the sun goes down…and we keep our eyes on Jesus anyway.

Maybe that's not what you want to hear. Verily, I say unto you, I don't like it much either. But that's the way it is. As the old saying goes, "It's better to light a candle than to curse the darkness."

What we need to do here, then, is to start developing a practical action plan for how to convert your crisis into opportunity. For the remainder of this chapter, I want to walk you through some specific ways to fan the flame of your audacious faith when the sun goes down. Again, there is no magic formula or answer key for this way of life. But I'm absolutely confident that when you see every crisis in your life as an opportunity to trust Christ more deeply, you will see the glory and goodness of God shining in and through your life.

THE OPPORTUNITY OF ADVERSITY

I can tell this is going to be a hard sell. Anytime you start juxtaposing words like *adversity* with *opportunity,* it kicks hard against common sense and conventional thinking. Don't you typically think of adversity as the opposite of opportunity? I usually pray for God to *remove* all the obstacles and opposition in my life. To my way of thinking, adversity gets in the way of opportunity.

But God doesn't think like I think. I guess that's why he rarely asks me what I think. So instead of *taking away* our adversity, he develops our faith and demonstrates his strength by *working through* our adversity.

I mean, if we're going to follow Joshua's example, we've got to follow it all the way from start to finish. We can't just copy his prayer. We must have his heart. We've got to take all his surrounding circumstances into consideration. And Joshua didn't pray that God would intervene miraculously in his day so he could have a few extra hours by the pool on the last day of spring break. He commanded the sun to stand still in the heat of battle. He was engaged in bloody combat, fighting to uphold the glory of the God of Israel. He wouldn't have needed the sun to stand still if he didn't have an enemy of God to defeat.

If you never faced an enemy of God, you would never experience God's victory. Where there is no opposition, there is no opportunity.

Have you ever thought about how dull some of the best-loved Bible stories would be if you cut out the crisis moments? Just for kicks, let's try it.

In a previous chapter I talked about one of Joshua's most formative faith experiences: the deliverance of God's people from Egyptian slavery. I showed you how, just before their great escape, Moses gave a stirring pep talk to the children of Israel.

> Moses answered the people, "Do not be afraid. Stand firm
> and you will see the deliverance the LORD will bring you
> today. The Egyptians you see today you will never see again."
> (Exodus 14:13)

Awesome. God is going to bring his people out of slavery and eliminate their enemies. Do you remember how dramatically he did it? Yeah, well, we're going to skip that part for now. Instead, we'll go right to the last frame: the happy ending.

> Then Moses led Israel from the Red Sea and they went into
> the Desert of Shur. (15:22)

Something seems to be missing. Namely, the part where the Egyptian army chased after the children of Israel, terrifying them within an inch of their lives. Oh, and the scene where God paved a four-lane highway through the Red Sea and blew back the waters to provide safe passage for his people. Followed by the grand finale—when God released the waves and drowned every single enemy who stood opposed to his purpose. God wanted his people to never forget the meaning of those crisis moments: *I've got your back. I'm present with you. I'm fighting for you. I'll never fail you.*

It's one of the most important stories in the history of God's activity on earth. And how did it begin? With a crisis. Because of a battle. In the thick of adversity.

All the good stories start with adversity. All our favorite plot lines are made up of major conflict. Of course, we wouldn't choose to write *our own* stories that way. We want *our* stories to jump straight from the promise of deliverance to the after party in the Promised Land. We like to watch *other* people cross through the middle of the Red Sea with an evil empire closing in. But we'd prefer for God to build a bridge over our troubled waters—and destroy our enemies before they get within striking distance.

It doesn't work that way. It can't work that way. Because you'd never see how strong God is if there were no opponent for him to overcome in your life.

THROW THE FIRST PUNCH
AND DON'T STOP SWINGING

I'm not suggesting that you pick a fight with the devil. I'm not advising you to invite pain and suffering into your life. And you won't have to. Adversity is inevitable. I'm simply saying that when the battle begins, you've got two options. You can stand there and get beaten to a bloody pulp, abandon your faith, and curse the day you were born. Or you can seize the opportunity to experience God's power and goodness in a new way, watching in awe as he fights for you.

My dad gave me some fighting tips while I was trying to survive junior high. Listen in. This is heartwarming stuff. "Son, nobody really wants to fight. But sometimes you don't have any other options. So the moment you realize that a fight is unavoidable, throw the first punch. Not even the U.S. Army can beat an ambush. And don't stop swinging until the fight is over."

I'm not sure my dad's suggestion would gain support at Focus on the Family. But it helped me deal with a lot of bullies over the years. And it's a fitting analogy for how to manage the spiritual warfare we're sure to face as we live for God with audacious faith.

Throw the first punch. Seize the opportunity to see God fight for you rather than let your adversary destroy you blow by blow.

And don't stop swinging. Don't give up. Don't compromise or abandon your faith the first time things don't go your way. Or even if certain things *never* go your way.

God didn't send Jesus to throw in the towel and call off all our fights. God sent Jesus to step into the ring and fight our battles.

I don't know what kind of enemies you'll have to engage as you fight the fight of audacious faith. You may have to demonstrate the patience of Job and the compassion of Christ toward a rebellious teenager. You may have to press through chronic physical pain, wondering why God has healed so many other people but won't heal you.

I'm only thirty years old. Maybe I haven't had to fight nearly as many adversaries as you have. Maybe you think I can't relate to your particular level of pain. And you may be right. But I've had a ringside seat to watch some godly people go all twelve rounds with crippling circumstances. And they were still standing strong in faith at the end.

PAPA'S GRAND FINALE

My grandfather Thomas Liles—we called him Papa—is one of my all-time heroes of the faith. He was a really good man. He's not listed in the Hebrews 11 Hall of Faith alongside Jacob. He never made the sun stand still like Joshua. But he taught me more about audacious faith than any other man I've ever known. He stayed faithful to Jesus through the darkest night of his life, even though his dark night lasted more than ten years: Papa watched helplessly as his wife of over fifty years lost her mind and body to Alzheimer's disease.

Papa begged God daily for a miracle. And he had every right to. He had served the Lord faithfully as a Methodist minister for more than three decades. He had been counselor and comforter for hundreds of families over the years in the darkest moments of *their* lives. Papa had been true to my grandmother for over a half century. He provided for his family, loved his kids, and for a lifetime he had stayed faithful to the assignment God had given him. My mom said she *never once* heard him raise his voice in anger or speak a negative word about someone else behind his back. So surely Papa was a prime candidate for a Sun Stand Still miracle. Surely, in the darkest moment in *his* life, God would grant him his simple request for the healing of the woman he loved.

Yet no answer came.

Every morning he'd arrive at the nursing home as the sun came up so that he could be the first visitor on the premises. He would sit by his wife's bed day after day, hour after hour, even though it rarely even registered with her that he was there. She had lost all ability to connect on a meaningful level. I remember how sad and disturbing it felt to look into her eyes and see how empty they were. And tired. She had given up.

But Papa wouldn't give up. He held on to faith. He never left her side. I'll never forget the smell of the nursing home. Or the sight of my grandfather kneeling by his wife's bedside, combing her hair, telling her she was beautiful. She couldn't remember his name, but he never stopped praying, believing, and loving. He kept walking in faith.

And yet the sun kept sinking. My grandmother's condition got downright disgusting. I was a teenager at the time and could hardly believe what I was hearing: "Grandma woke up in the middle of the night cursing at Papa and trying to find a knife because she was convinced somebody was coming to get her," or, "Grandma went to the bathroom all over herself again, and she won't let them clean her."

This wasn't the Grandma I had known growing up. Virginia Liles was cheerful, tidy, proper, spunky—a professional educator, the consummate pastor's wife, and the best grandma ever. It was nauseating to see her bloated, beaten down, and belligerent.

I can't imagine what it was like for Papa. I think he must have peeked through the curtains each morning with a little less hope than he'd had the day before.

And the sky kept getting darker. Her condition continued to deteriorate. She wouldn't eat. She wouldn't leave her room.

Papa died about eighteen months before Grandma passed

away. The final scenes of their marriage were pitiful, really, from a purely earthly perspective. Healing never came. And it broke Papa's heart. In fact, it broke the hearts of everyone who cared about these two incredible Christian people.

I'm sure you've seen—or even tasted for yourself—similar situations. Maybe the sun has gone down on an ambition in your life recently, and you can't shake the pain of the failure. The business went under, leaving you depleted and demoralized. Maybe someone you thought you couldn't live without chose to leave your life, and the reality that you'll never get her back makes you feel like life isn't worth living anymore. Maybe you've disappointed yourself and everyone you care about. You're not even sure if you have the faith, the energy, or the second wind to pray.

I'm glad my grandfather didn't lose his faith, even when the sun went down and he lost what mattered most to him. Even though almost nothing good happened to him for the last decade of his life, I'm grateful that he stayed true to his belief that God is good. I'm grateful that he set a standard of marriage for me that I will not only live by and pass on to my boys, but also share with thousands in our own church and all across the world.

Sometimes God has to let the sun go down so that his glory can shine through our lives. The darker it gets in your situation, the brighter God in his goodness and grace can shine through you for the world to see.

I have the audacious faith to believe that my grandparents have crossed over into a new and improved reality. Nothing is missing. Nothing is broken. All things are made new in the eternal presence of Jesus.

The sun may have gone down for a little while. But when we

see the time line of our trials in the light of eternity, the pain lasts only a moment. Paul put it this way in 2 Corinthians 4:17:

> Our light and momentary troubles are achieving for us an eternal glory that far outweighs them all.

Sometimes God will make the sun stand still. You'll get what you pray for and then some. When he does, be thankful. Give him all the credit. Ride the wave of blessing as far as it will take you.

But there are guaranteed to be *other* times. God may occasionally choose to let the sun go down. The money won't get there in time. The relationship will get more unbearable. The condition will deteriorate. The dream will die.

Standing in this darkness, what should you do?

BE THE MIRACLE

Listen, no one but you and God really knows what you're going through right now. But with all my heart, I urge you, trust your heavenly Father. Stand still and see his strength as he fights for you.

I heard a wise, older pastor say it this way: "Sometimes we get to see the miracle; other times we get to be the miracle." In other words, sometimes God's strength is demonstrated in what he does *around* us—the external effects of our faith and tangible answers to our prayers. Other times his strength shines *in* us, enabling us to endure devastating setbacks with remarkable strength.

I'm glad Joshua didn't quit in the wilderness. I'm glad he endured forty brutal years of aimless wandering, marching to the beat of incessant backbiting and second-guessing, bitterness and grumbling. He chose to believe that the sun can't stay down forever. And a new day dawned for Joshua. God raised him up to depose kings and lead people at a level that would make the previous forty years seem like the blink of an eye—okay, a really long, agonizing blink. But he found the faith to pray again. He chose to believe that God could *still* make the sun stand still.

I'm glad God didn't cut the crisis moments out of the Bible. Without them, we would know nothing of his power. We would have nothing on which to base our trust in his unlimited provision. We would never prove his potential. We would never be carried by his tender mercies or have stories to tell of his presence in our darkest hours.

Sometimes God lets the sun go down so that he can be our only light.

Audacious faith doesn't mean my prayers work every time. It means that God is working even when my prayers don't seem to be working at all.

And I choose to believe that audacious faith enables me to seize the opportunity in my adversity. Seize the opportunity in my scarcity to wait for God's unfailing provision. Seize the opportunity in my uncertainty to trust in God's good purposes for me.

Remember that your crisis is your greatest opportunity to see God's glory and goodness revealed—and to have the high honor of revealing him to others.

CHAPTER 14

Pray Like a Juggernaut

A few years ago, I started realizing that I prayed some pretty dumb prayers. Not that I think God needs me to be eloquent or profound when I talk to him. It's just that a lot of the stuff I was praying was, well, rather pointless and obtuse. Here are a couple of examples from *Furtick's Book of Dumb Prayers*.

See if you can relate to this one: *God, just be with me today.*

Now, before you go getting all insulted (because I know you've prayed this one yourself), let me say right here that I understand the heart behind this prayer. And I'm sure God does too. What we *mean* is that we want to experience his presence and power in our lives. But come on. Isn't the prayer *God, just be with me today* usually just filler? The kind of prayer we pray because we know we need to pray but we don't really know *what* to say? Or we really don't want to commit to anything specific, so we just keep it comfortably vague?

God fills heaven and earth. Every inch on this planet, and every other planet, belongs to him. And if we're believers in Jesus, God lives in us in the form of the Holy Spirit. Do we really need to make sure he's going to *be with us*? Couldn't we get a little more creative?

Or how about this one? I used to always prequalify my big prayers with this introduction: *God, if it be thy will…*

So, does God need an opt-out clause in the contract before he's willing to sign on the line and cut a deal with Steven Furtick? or with you? Again, I think we tack this on without thinking. We don't mean any harm. It sounds good, doesn't it? It's even got a little King James English flair—which we all know makes the prayer more official. And on the surface, this whole idea seems very humble.

Over time, though, I realized that I wasn't buffering my prayers with this condition because I was humble. I was doing it because I was scared. When I started with *God, if it be thy will…*, it made whatever I prayed about next feel safer. So, actually, it was a cop-out. What I was really praying was, *God, I'm asking you to do this, but I'm not really expecting that you will. So, just in case you don't, let me acknowledge up front that you might not.*

How about you? Prayed any dumb prayers lately? Don't you get tired of lobbing empty language out into the atmosphere, hoping it materializes into something good? Would you believe me if I told you that audacious faith introduces a whole new way to approach your prayer life…and you can turn it around today?

A LARGE, OVERPOWERING FORCE IN MOTION

When it comes to prayer, a lot of us have the standard stuff down. We can string together enough spiritual-sounding words to hold our own if called upon in public. But praying a Sun Stand Still prayer requires something more than general competence. It takes us into new, unfamiliar, often intimidating territory. It isn't like asking God to give you a good parking spot when you're late for church or to bless your pepperoni pizza to the nourishment of your body. A Sun Stand Still prayer is wrapped with urgency. It's filled with possibility. And for most of us, it's a whole new way to pray.

I call it praying like a juggernaut. A juggernaut is defined as "a massive inexorable force, campaign, movement, or object that crushes whatever is in its path." It's often used to describe an unstoppable movement. I like that image. A lot. Maybe this is my testosterone talking, but when it comes to prayer, I don't think it gets any better than that. And when it comes to identifying a model for praying this way, I can't think of a more unstoppable juggernaut than our man Joshua.

Joshua's Sun Stand Still prayer is not something we simply admire. Simple as it is, it shows us a bold way to address God that we can emulate. And this is true of all the great prayers of the Bible. They're recorded in Scripture to set an all-time prayer standard for us. To force us out of our defensive prayer posture. To inspire us to rise up and begin to pray...like juggernauts.

Juggernauts like Moses, who stood in God's way and prayed that God wouldn't kill the Israelites after they worshiped the golden calf.

Juggernauts like the apostles, who asked for and expected miracles, and who spoke out boldly in the face of persecution so that the name of Jesus could be lifted high.

Juggernauts like Elijah, whose prayer both caused and ended a three-and-a-half-year drought.

You may push back on this, but I suggest that the prayers of these people are not abnormal. They are not the exception. At least they were never meant to be. The tragedy of our time is that we have taken what was meant to be ordinary and made it exceptional. We've put audacity on the highest shelf, out of reach, and declared it off limits. James 5:17 makes this eye-opening statement:

> Elijah was a man just like us. He prayed earnestly that it would not rain, and it did not rain on the land for three and a half years.

It's too bad that most of us focus on the second part of this verse. We're stunned by the superior power of Elijah's prayer life. We'd love to have an ounce of his power flowing in our prayer lives. But we don't have to wish. That's the whole point of this passage. We *are* just like Elijah. We *are* just like Joshua.

Think about it. Elijah had access to an all-powerful God who could stop the rain. We have access to an all-powerful God who can stop the rain. Joshua had access to an all-powerful God who could make the sun stand still. We have access to an all-powerful God who can make the sun stand still. The only difference is that Elijah and Joshua had the audacity to pray prayers that lived up to God's character, God's heart, God's resources, God's will, and God's abilities.

That's what it means to pray like a juggernaut: to pray prayers worthy of the God we're praying to. After all, we're praying to a God whose capability always exceeds our audacity. You don't have to worry about ever putting God in an awkward or embarrassing position. You're not going to back him into a corner. You won't ever challenge him to do something beyond his aptitude.

Prayer is the arena where our faith meets God's abilities. And there is never going to be a moment when the audacity of our faith surpasses God's capacity to respond. That's why timid prayers are a waste of time. Is it really worthy of our God to ask him for a *good day* as our main point of conversation with him every morning? Or to ask him to make our job more tolerable? You and I are called to pray *beyond* that. Not just that God would give us a good day, but that he would show us his greatness throughout the day. Not just that we will find the strength to tolerate our work, but that we will find a purpose that can drive us to excel in our jobs for his glory.

It may take some adjustment and coaching to get to a place where extraordinary prayers become ordinary in our lives. It may require that we flex some muscles we didn't know we had. But the Bible leaves us without excuse: We're strong in the Lord. And it's time to put those muscles to work.

I'm going to let you in on the simple approach that has incubated my audacious prayer life. It has given new life, new perspective, and a different dimension to my prayers. I've got to warn you, though—this is high-voltage stuff. Sun Stand Still prayers can generate some pretty radical results.

SUNSET ON THE LOADING DOCK

One of the most discouraging days of my pastoral career was the day in 2008 when our church was scheduled to sign a contract to occupy a forty-two-thousand-square-foot facility in a local shopping center. We had big plans to retrofit the space and turn it into a worship center. It was going to be our first permanent location and our new ministry headquarters. But at the last minute, one of the other tenants chose to exercise a clause in the lease to deny us occupancy. This particular company couldn't stand the thought of a church having worship services anywhere near its store. We pleaded. The tenant wouldn't budge.

So we prayed. Not like beggars. Like juggernauts. We loaded up a group of about a hundred hard-core Elevators (that's what we call our church members) and went to the facility that very night. We got down on our knees on the oil-stained loading docks behind the building and asked God to give us that property...in Jesus' name.

For a solid year, nothing happened.

Still, almost every day, when I drove by that building on my way to our offices, I just couldn't let it go. I sensed that this space was supposed to be ours. So I prayed. Every time I passed it. Out loud. I must have stretched my hand toward that warehouse three hundred times. And each time, I spoke these words of faith: "Father, I thank you that our church *will* have worship services in that warehouse and we *will* reach thousands of people for Jesus Christ, according to your perfect plan, in your perfect timing."

By September 2009, we were conducting worship services with thousands of people in that building. Not only that, but one Sunday evening we also had the opportunity to baptize a couple hundred people on the very same oil-stained loading docks where we had lifted our voices in bold prayer eighteen months earlier. I had chills throughout my body as I stood off to the side, taking in the baptisms with my whole family and staff by my side. The atmosphere of gratitude was absolutely electric. God had come through for us against all odds.

Oh, and if you're wondering what happened to the business that originally wouldn't let us in the building—it went bankrupt. Not just that one store. The whole chain. Seventy-seven stores nationwide. I'm not saying God put this company out of business. But it makes you wonder…

A large, powerful force in motion.

Unstoppable movement.

What a way to pray!

I hope I'm not freaking you out too badly here. Listen, I'm not advocating that we drive around praying for organizations to go out of business or waving our arms wildly, randomly claiming real estate.

But when it comes to standing on God's purposes and promises, why shouldn't we push the limits and aggressively pursue new territory? It's the approach taken by the great juggernauts of prayer in the amazing events recorded in the Bible. And it's the same approach that can enable you to become a juggernaut of prayer in our day.

I want to walk you through some of the specific qualities of Sun Stand Still prayers. When I'm finished, you'll have a pattern for building a case before God in prayer. Now, the first time I heard the phrase *build a case before God*, I didn't get it. It sounded like courtroom theology. It even seemed to have a manipulative vibe. I assure you, however, that building a case before God is biblical, and it's practical. And I've seen it transform the prayer lives of thousands of Christians who are tired of praying to God about the same old things in the same old way.

It's not enough to figure out *what* you need to pray about. But you might need some help knowing *how* to pray about what you know you need to pray about. And by building a case before God, you can approach him with audacious faith, because your prayer is based on a solid foundation.

RECONCILE YOUR DREAMS WITH GOD'S DESIRES

First John 5:14–15 is a classic juggernaut prayer passage:

> This is the confidence we have in approaching God: that if we ask anything according to his will, he hears us. And if we know that he hears us—whatever we ask—we know that we have what we asked of him.

Notice that it doesn't say "if we ask anything we desire" or "if we ask anything audaciously," but "if we ask anything *according to his will.*" In other words, God wants our agenda to align with his agenda. Our audacity must be in sync with God's purposes.

Praying this way reconciles your God-sized dreams with the God you actually find in the Bible. It makes you filter your audacity through God's desires, not just your own. And hopefully, over time, your desires and God's desires will become one and the same.

Please note: Praying with audacity does not mean you simply pray the biggest prayer you can think of that is going to benefit your life. You don't need much imagination to come up with this type of prayer. You could ask God to let you live the rest of your life free from physical and emotional pain. You could pray for billions of dollars to instantly hit your bank account. Hallelujah. Sun stand still. What's the magic word again?

These requests are audacious. But they're also self-obsessed and disconnected from reality. If your Sun Stand Still prayer isn't based on God's agenda in the world, you don't have much of a case to build. What you have, my friend, is a fantasy.

The last thing I want to do is stifle your prayers or make you afraid to pray the impossible. Just the opposite: I desperately desire for you to stop settling for the low-grade prayers that characterize the lives of far too many believers. But I also want to see your bold prayers answered as God moves in a mighty way in your life for his glory. That's not going to happen if you are praying only to benefit your own agenda.

This is why the Word of God is so crucial to audacious faith. It is impossible to separate audacious and effective prayer from knowledge of the Word of God. It is in the Word that we find God's promises and his pattern of acting in history. It is in the Word that our paradigms of thinking are reprogrammed to match God's purposes in our lives and the world. Every time you kneel before the Father to pray with audacity, you must have his Word in your mind and in your heart. Otherwise, you risk confusing your agenda with his, praying gigantic prayers that bring microscopic returns.

REMIND GOD OF WHAT HE ALREADY KNOWS

Joshua prayed that the sun would stand still because God had promised the Israelites to fight for them and defeat their enemies. Joshua's bold request was based on a promise God had made to him. He wanted to see God's purposes accomplished.

In Exodus 32, we read about how Moses found the courage to respond to God's threat to destroy the Israelites after they worshiped the golden calf by pointing out that it would defame his name in Egypt and by reminding him of a promise he had made to Abraham, Isaac, and Jacob. Moses' desire was to see God's name honored and his promise fulfilled, and this gave him the audacity to stand between God and the Israelites.

David spent the first half of Psalm 68 praising God for his past deeds of deliverance and salvation. But on the basis of this, he said in verse 28, "Show us your strength, O God, as you have done before." David knew God had delivered the Israelites from enemies in the past and therefore asked that God would do it in the present.

In each of these scenarios, one of God's servants is *reminding God* of something he did in the past or a promise he made concerning the future. What's up with that? Did God forget? Does he need an administrative assistant?

Reminding God of his promises isn't about giving him new information. It's about experiencing his transformation. By going back to the Word of God and recalling his promises and the pattern of his actions in the past, your audacity is stirred. Your desires are aligned with God's purposes. The promises of God are woven into the fabric of your faith. And your motivations become his motivations.

Let me show you how this works in our lives today.

Maybe you're facing a significant decision that will affect the entire direction of your life, and you don't know what to do next. Your Sun Stand Still prayer could start like this:

Lord, I read in Genesis 12 how you told Abraham to go to the land that you would show him. He didn't know what the final destination would be, but he acted in obedience to what you had said. And you led him step by step along the way. So, Lord, right now I don't know what the final destination is going to be for me, but I'm going to take the next step that you've told me to take. God, like you led

Abraham back then, would you lead me now? Would you give me wisdom? Would you show me the next right thing to do?

Or maybe you are married and have been unable to have children. Your Sun Stand Still prayer may begin with this:

Lord, my spouse and I desperately want to raise godly children who will be leaders in their generation for your glory. I was reading in the Bible about a woman named Hannah. She was really bitter and sad because she didn't have a child. She prayed to you, and you gave her the desire of her heart. And she dedicated that child to you. Lord, I'm asking that you would send a child into our lives. As you do, I promise to give you the glory and the praise. I want this to be all about you, so if you say no to that, I trust that you're wiser than I am, because I have built this prayer on the foundation of your sovereignty, not my preferences or my own agenda. But God, in accordance with what you've done for others, would you do it for me?

Or let's say you have a shortage of money or assets, and you desperately need God to provide for your family. Instead of going to God and pleading with him on the basis of *pretty please, God...,* go to him and say:

Lord, I'm low on resources. One time I read in Matthew 14 how you fed over five thousand people with five loaves and two fish. God, would you multiply that same kind of provision for my family right now?

It's remarkable to realize that you can pray this way about anything—the healing of an illness, the salvation of the lost, reconciliation in torn-apart families, the lifting of depression, the homecoming of children who have wandered, and everything else under the sun. Building a case before God is so much better than resorting to prayers that begin like this: *Lord, would you please send us some money? I mean, if you don't want to, it's all good. If it be thy will...*

Discard the disclaimers. Stop hunting and pecking to find the will of God. Go to the Scriptures and *know* God's will.

When you pray according to God's promises, you will be praying God's will. Like I said earlier, you don't have to prequalify all your prayers. In 1 John 5:14, the Bible says that if you ask anything according to his will, he hears you. It's time to speak up with a bold, new confidence.

Building a case before God in prayer is dangerous. If done right, it has the power to actually change the fundamental structures of your life and the world. But if you get this concept twisted, you could end up asking for what you deserve. And in this case, that's the worst possible approach you could take.

You Don't Want What You Deserve

I don't want to expose you to the concept of building a case in prayer without clarifying exactly what kind of case you're building. Otherwise, you might put down this book and start to pray:

> *Lord, I consider myself a good person. You know I've been working really hard. I've been serving you all my life. My back's against the wall on this one. I need you to come through in a huge way. God, I'm doing the best I can. Now can you hook a brother up?*

Let me assure you: When you come before God, the last thing you want to do is build your case on the basis of what you think you deserve. I promise you—you don't want what you deserve.

That last statement goes against the grain of what our culture and even what many Christians believe. Most believe that if people are good, or at least try to be good, they deserve certain good things from God. They deserve to be blessed. They deserve to be happy. And they definitely deserve to have their prayers answered. The problem is that this belief is based on a notion that God is keeping our spiritual credit score, and his response to us is based on the quality of our performance. In reality, when we come before God and start building a case on the basis of *our* credit, we're setting ourselves up for disappointment.

When I was in tenth grade, I had a social studies teacher who was also a football coach. He was definitely more coach than teacher. So he wasn't in class much during football season. He showed a lot of videos. I appreciated that. It made for my favorite kind of class—the kind I didn't have to think about much.

When we got our first progress report, I was surprised to notice that I had a C in Coach's class. Certainly I didn't *deserve* a C. I took my case straight to the coach. He was cool. He was laid-back. He liked me. Surely we could work something out.

"Coach," I said, "what's up with this C you gave me?"

He studied my face. It seemed like he was trying to feel me out. Finally he said, "I don't know. Let's get out the grade book and take a look."

He opened up the grade book. I noticed a lot of zeros in the homework column. I never imagined in my wildest dreams that he was actually keeping track of the homework that I wasn't turning in. Obviously, I had underestimated him. Coach pulled out a calculator and started calculating all the other grades. The result was a C. Then he averaged in all the zeros. As he summed up the situation, he put the grade book down and looked at me squarely.

"You know, Steven, you're right," he said calmly. "You're absolutely right. You don't deserve a C in my class. Not at all. Looks like you deserve an F. Would you like me to make the adjustment?"

Suddenly that C seemed more than fair. In fact, it seemed downright gracious.

I sat back down and shut my mouth. So much for what I *deserved*.

We've got to realize that if God ever really broke out the calculator and the grade book, *none* of our prayers would be answered. No one is qualified to come before God. None of us have built up enough credit or goodwill to enable us to be in any way entitled to get God to move.

Don't ever ask God to give you the grade you deserve. True prayers of faith are based in grace. Build your case on this: the righteousness that has been credited to your account through the perfect performance of Jesus Christ.

Sun Stand Still prayers aren't about changing God's mind. They're about changing your heart, activating your faith, and developing your confidence in God's Word and character. As this happens, the audacity of your prayers will increase because you will repeatedly encounter a God who has acted audaciously in the past and longs to do so today.

He still longs to make the sun stand still. In the past, it was a juggernaut named Joshua who acted on that promise. Now it's your turn.

CHAPTER 15

Permission to Pray Practically

God is interested in every single area of your life. It's not like the only time you can pray a Sun Stand Still prayer is on the front lines of the mission field, when you're building orphanages or translating the Bible into new languages.

So in case you haven't already started thinking through some of the personal needs, longings, hopes, and dreams that seem impossible to you, or in case you aren't sure what's allowed, I want to give you some guidance here.

In chapter 4, I gave you a list of areas in your life you might pray a Sun Stand Still prayer about. But I want to delve a little deeper into some of the seemingly impossible personal needs that warrant this kind of faith-filled prayer. Your results may not be exactly the same as those of the people I mention. But you can embrace the spirit of their faith. And you have every reason to believe that God can work the same way in your life.

I've seen couples who struggled with infertility pray Sun Stand Still prayers that God would allow them to get pregnant. Many of them went on to have healthy babies. They trace the impetus of their miracle back to the Sun Stand Still prayer they prayed. They talk a lot about the faith it took to keep their vision in sight while the doctors kept telling them they'd never conceive.

I've also seen many couples battle infertility and pray Sun Stand Still prayers only to see zero progress in their physical condition after months of hoping, believing, and trying. Many of these couples took that as a sign that God wanted them to become parents through adoption, and they stepped out in faith to begin the process. Most of them would tell you, "God still answered our Sun Stand Still prayer. He just did it in his own creative way."

A lot of people pray Sun Stand Still prayers about their careers. I wholeheartedly endorse this. My friend Mike was inspired by the idea of activating a Page 23 vision for his business. He started meeting with his six employees to explore what a Sun Stand Still prayer would look like in their industry. Since Mike's company manages people's money, his Sun Stand Still prayer is a little tricky. After all, a lot of Christians believe that earning large sums of money is completely unrelated to accomplishing God's purposes. Mike doesn't see it that way. Although he knows that believers should never put their hope in wealth, he's decided to leverage his skills to generate financial increase for God's glory. So his Sun Stand Still prayer is to enrich and impact lives by being one of the greatest money managers in his generation and by building a world-class team centered on biblical principles.

The result? Mike has experienced a lot of success making a lot of money for a lot of people. He gives a sizable percentage of his profits back to the cause of Christ worldwide. And he impacts and enriches the lives of the hundreds of people he works with.

Financial and physical needs often inspire Sun Stand Still prayers. Can you really pray about these things? Absolutely. I've seen God directly answer prayers for provision and healing more times than I can count. Of course, he doesn't do it the same way every time. And we can't reduce this thing to a formula, claiming that he always does this or that when we pray a certain way. Still, the same Jesus who touched hurting people and created miraculous supply when he walked this earth can work in our lives just as dramatically today.

Your specific Sun Stand Still need may not be represented by the stories I've just shared. That's okay. The idea isn't to give you a checklist. I just want to give you permission to pray about your needs according to God's will with full confidence that he cares about *all* the impossible needs in your life—in every single area of your life.

So go ahead: Pray. Pray imaginatively. Pray unstoppably.

And expect a miracle.

CHAPTER 16

Sweet Southern Audacity

A while back, when we were digging through some old stuff in our house, my wife, Holly, and I came across a cassette tape marked *Steven 18 Months Old.* After we finally located a piece of ancient technology known as a cassette player, we had a good time listening to the tape.

Apparently this recording had been made at my Aunt Jackie's house when I was a little boy. For most of the tape, Aunt Jackie is trying to get me to eat some peas, and I am telling her that I want her to turn on the radio. After about twelve rounds of this, she gives in and turns on the radio, and you can hear me kind of singing along—as much as an eighteen-month-old can sing along. That tape triggered some vivid memories in my mind. Memories of the days when we had cassette tapes, for one thing (my favorite being *Led Zeppelin IV*). Good memories, man.

But the more profound memories were about Aunt Jackie. Aunt Jackie is still going pretty strong at age eighty-three. She's still living in Moncks Corner, South Carolina, in the same house where she's lived for over forty years. She's still attending the same church and serving on the same committees she's served on most of her life. She's Methodist to the bone, and when my mom listed all the behind-the-scenes positions she's held at the Methodist church where I grew up, I wondered how astronomical her back-pay would be if she had earned even minimum wage for every hour she had volunteered.

Aunt Jackie is a really sweet, selfless, servant-hearted Southern woman, though she's capable of getting in your face when the circumstances call for it. Oh, and she technically isn't my aunt. She's not related to me at all actually. But I've called her Aunt Jackie as long as I can remember. I used to get to go to her house all the time when I was a boy. She didn't have kids of her own, because she never married. Her parents suffered from chronic illnesses, and she felt that God was calling her to devote her life to taking care of them.

Since Aunt Jackie didn't have any children, she totally spoiled me and my brother. That meant we really liked being at her house. She let us watch *The Dukes of Hazzard*. I say she *let us* watch it, as if she were making some kind of sacrifice. But my mom says Aunt Jackie really just liked watching Bo and Luke. Our being there gave her an excuse.

The reason I mention Aunt Jackie to you, though, isn't to analyze her TV-viewing habits. I want to hold up Aunt Jackie's life as an example of audacious faith.

If Aunt Jackie knew I was writing about how audacious she is, she'd laugh her head off. If she knew I was comparing her to Joshua, she'd probably veto this chapter.

But looking back over my life, it's obvious that Aunt Jackie is one of the most audacious people I've ever known.

Here's why. Not only has she made difficult sacrifices to take care of others, trusting God to take care of her, with no concern for her own glory…not only has she been a bedrock of the small Methodist congregation my grandfather used to pastor, making sure the flowers were always fresh and the fellowship hall was always clean…but also Aunt Jackie is a mighty warrior in prayer.

I know that she has prayed some serious Sun Stand Still prayers over the course of her life—and I'm sure there are many more that I don't know about. But one Sun Stand Still prayer she prayed is deeply meaningful to me…because I'm pretty sure it's one of the reasons I'm sharing this message with you today.

I was sixteen years old, and it had been three months or so since I'd given my life to Christ. Aunt Jackie stopped me in the church parking lot one Wednesday night after choir practice and gave me a hug, like she always did. She told me she didn't like my hair, which was dyed orange at the time, but other than that, I looked very handsome, and she was proud of me, and she couldn't believe how tall I was. And then she told me that she had something important to say, and I needed to hear it.

"Steven, God has a special plan for you."

"Thanks, Aunt Jackie. I really apprecia—"

"Steven, be quiet and listen to me for a minute. You don't have to talk all the time, son."

"Yes ma'am."

"Now, I was saying that God has a special plan for your life. And I know that, son, because I've been watching you and praying for you all your life. And God told me that he's going to use you to change the world. Do you believe that, Steven?"

"Um, yes ma'am. I think I can see what you're say—"

"Well, whether you believe it or not, it's true. God always gets his way, and I am praying that you'll be one of God's greatest instruments to get the Word out."

I had no idea at the time what a Sun Stand Still prayer was. Or that I'd have the opportunity to share this message with people all over the world. But Aunt Jackie, in her own Southern, Methodist, audacious way, was praying a Sun Stand Still prayer over my life and believing for God to do the impossible through me.

Maybe the greatest Sun Stand Still prayers God will answer over the course of your life will be the audacious prayers of faith you pray for *others*. Maybe no one will even know you prayed them. Maybe you'll never see the connection between what you prayed for someone else and what God does in the other person's life years down the road.

But I can tell you this much. From God's perspective, every time I preach a sermon, write a book, and touch a life, there's a little woman from Moncks Corner, South Carolina, whose heavenly account is accumulating interest.

Don't underestimate the people like Aunt Jackie who don't look anything like Joshua on the surface but who shake things up through a lifetime of consistent prayer.

She never could get me to eat my peas. But her prayers prepared a way for me to make a difference in the world.

CHAPTER 17

Push While You Pray

My firstborn son, Elijah, was born the normal way. Not a single complication. He did go on to cry for the entire first year of his life. But the actual delivery process was silky smooth.

Our second son, Graham, made a more dramatic entrance. A week before Graham's due date, the doctors decided to induce Holly. And Holly had already determined that epidural anesthesia was among God's greatest gifts and that she would be utilizing it fully. So we arrived at the hospital at a convenient time, got the process started, and settled in like old pros.

Holly was sipping on ginger ale, watching a rerun of *The Cosby Show*, when a nurse came in and started doing her nurse thing. I asked her, for the fifth or sixth time that day, how long it would be before Holly needed to start pushing. According to the last update, it was three hours. But this time the nurse didn't answer. If she was annoyed, I understood, but since that has never deterred me, I asked again. She gave me a look that said, *Shut up, Big Daddy. I've got more important concerns than your curiosity right now.*

So I shut up. Then I watched as she called another nurse into the room. Then a doctor. Then two more nurses. Then another doctor. Then a tech came in pushing a big machine they didn't use when Elijah was born. Everybody looked really serious, and I was starting to get concerned.

"What's going on?" I asked in all the commotion. "Can somebody please tell me what's up? I need to know if everything's okay."

The main doctor gave me a calm but measured reply. "Dad," he said, "you need to calm down. We've got a complication. We can't talk to you right now. Right now, the most important thing is that we help your wife push."

He turned to Holly. "Mrs. Furtick, it's time to push."

Holly started to cry and launched into her own set of questions about what in the world was going on.

The doctor gave her an abbreviated version of the speech I'd just heard. "No questions, ma'am. This isn't the time. This is the time to push. Here we go."

She started pushing. About ten minutes later, Graham was born. But when he came out, he was purple. Turns out the umbilical cord had gotten wrapped around his neck. The monitors had been showing that he wasn't getting enough oxygen. That's why they had all showed up so suddenly.

Thankfully, within ten minutes of his arrival, Graham recovered completely. We were grateful but still in shock. They told us that it was all standard procedure for them, that the complication happens quite often. For me, the experience was abnormal and traumatic. Probably the scariest ten minutes of my life.

As they began to file out, I thanked the doctors and nurses for ignoring my questions and taking care of my wife. They looked at me as if to say, *We're glad to have your approval, buddy.*

Of course, the next night Holly was emotionally and physically exhausted and desperately trying to get some sleep. I sat up late in her room, working and reflecting on the whole experience. It wasn't like there was even a remote chance I would sleep on the standard-issue torture rack the hospital provided for dads. Plus, because of poor planning, I had to preach the next day. I was making a few final notes. My passage was Joshua 10, the chapter where Joshua commands the sun to stand still. (Ever heard of that one?)

This time, though, I was studying the events that led up to the solar miracle. And in light of all the drama we'd just been through, right there in that hospital room, I was struck by something I'd missed before. Let me describe the sequence.

First, there's God's sweeping promise to Joshua:

> Do not be afraid of them; I have given them into your hand.
> Not one of them will be able to withstand you. (verse 8)

Two verses later we see God start to fulfill his own promise. Enemy soldiers flee. Israel gives chase. God joins in by hurling down hailstones on the fleeing Amorites.

And a couple of verses after that, Joshua prays his epic, sun-stopping prayer.

But hold up a minute. Between the promise and the miracle comes an easy-to-overlook piece of information:

> After an all-night march from Gilgal, Joshua took them by surprise. (verse 9)

An all-night march? Lugging weapons and supplies through enemy territory in the dark? Twenty miles *uphill* (scholars tell us) only hours before the biggest battle of the campaign?

Wow.

Suddenly I had a flash of insight about prayer.

If you're going to pray for God to make the sun stand still, you'd better be ready to march all night.

Joshua's big prayer wasn't a cop-out. He didn't ask God to make the sun stand still while kneeling in the comfort of his tent. He did it on his feet after an all-night march.

Joshua did all he could, from a natural perspective. He applied himself physically, leading thousands of soldiers on what had to be a grueling nighttime march. He applied himself mentally, strategically executing the march beneath the cloak of darkness to ambush the enemy.

Then he asked God to add the *super* to his *natural*. And God obliged.

Supernatural Sun Stand Still faith, as I noted earlier, isn't divorced from our actions. In fact, these familiar words from James started making more sense to me than ever before:

Faith by itself, if it is not accompanied by action, is dead. (2:17)

If you're going to have the audacity to ask God for something, you'd better be ready to act. Audacious prayer must be tethered to practical obedience. Or else it's not faith. It's just wishful thinking and positive mental energy. No wonder so many of our prayers aren't answered. We pray for a miracle, but we fail to make a move.

And most of the time, if you don't move, God won't move. That's just the way he designed faith to work.

In light of this new revelation, I replayed Graham's delivery in my mind. But I reconstructed it from an absurd perspective. What if, I imagined, the doctor had discovered that my child wasn't getting any oxygen, and when I asked what was going on, he stopped treating my wife? And what if, after he stopped, he instructed the technicians to disconnect all the machines and the nurses to stop their procedures? And what if he told everyone to take a knee and then started explaining: "Folks, this is bad. If we don't get this baby out in the next few minutes, he'll either die or suffer permanent damage. This is really bad. So we need to pray, okay? Everybody stop what you're doing for the next few minutes, and let's all go around in a circle and pray. Let's pray for the baby, let's pray for the mom, let's pray for the equipment and for each medical professional in this room, by name. Let's just stop and pray, in Jesus' name."

I would have interrupted the doctor. I would have said (or more likely shouted) something like this: "Doctor, I appreciate your faith. But if you're telling me that my baby might die if we don't get him out right now, we're going to get him out *right now*! Nobody believes in prayer more than I do. But right now, you're going to hook the machines back up and put your gloves back on. We're not going to stop and pray. We're going to push—and we'll pray while we're doing it."

People who walk in audacious faith don't stop and pray. Audacious faith teaches us to push and pray.

ALL WE CAN DO IS PRAY?

Sometimes you'll hear someone share about an urgent, dire need and then sign off with a note of desperation: "Well, all we can do is pray."

That makes me cringe. First of all, it makes prayer sound like a refuge of last resort. Or like prayer is the last kid picked for dodge ball. It's as if we are thinking, *We've tried all the other stuff, the effective stuff. Now I guess we'll pray.*

We should never reduce prayer to the realm of *it's all we can do.* Sometimes it is. But not as often as we think. And it's the passive-by-default attitude that drives me crazy. It makes prayer out to be puny, maybe even pointless.

But it also suggests a false dichotomy in the way God works. That line of thinking suggests that we should pray, then wait. If God wants to do it, he'll do it. If he doesn't, maybe we'll pray some more. But that's all we can do. All we can do is pray.

Prayer is rarely all we can do. We can pray *and* we can prepare. We can ask God to intervene *and* we can initiate changes in our lives to make it happen. We can ask the Lord to fight for us *and* we can pull out our swords and start fighting in his strength. Sun Stand Still prayers are integrated prayers: They join our faith-filled prayer with our faith-filled action. Joshua had the audacity to ask *and* the persistence to pursue.

If you're going to ask God to make the sun stand still, you'd better be ready to march all night.

If you're going to ask God to give you a better marriage, you need to start marching in that direction. Start speaking more kindly to your spouse. Start sowing seeds of encouragement, and stop being so sharp and rude and demoralizing. Invest time and money in dating each other again. Say you're sorry for the way you've neglected her. Apologize for making him feel stupid every time he shares an idea with you. Push while you pray.

If you're praying a Sun Stand Still prayer for a new job, you'd better be cleaning up your résumé. You shouldn't be sleeping in and waiting on God to send you a job. It probably won't be delivered to the front door of your apartment. You should be out looking for the job that you believe God has for you. Have the audacity to iron your shirt. Polish your shoes. Make some calls. Engage your creativity. Get involved in your miracle. Push while you pray.

If your Sun Stand Still prayer is that God would help you become debt free, great. Get out the calculator and the credit card bills. Meet with an expert. Pray while you crunch numbers. I'm serious. Make debt reduction a spiritual activity. Repent of your wrong spending as you assess the damage. Pray for self-control as you incorporate new habits. Don't wait for God to erase the hard drives of all the computers at American Express headquarters worldwide or to send an anonymous millionaire to settle your accounts. Pay down your balance at the same time you're praying about your situation. Push while you pray.

Have you got the rhythm?

Push, push, pray. Push, push, pray.

Sun stand still!

March all night.

God, please bless my children!

Spend time with them affirming their gifts and shepherding their hearts.

God, send me a good Christian wife!

Stop going to the club on Thursday night. Your good Christian girl isn't there. Get involved in a church. Be a man of God. Join the greeter team. Keep your eyes open.

God, help me lose weight.

Put down the doughnut. Exercise. Repeat.

I'm not saying God needs us to help him out. It's not like he's lifting something heavy, wheezing and wondering, *Can I get somebody to give me a hand over here?* As we've already seen, God is infinitely strong and capable. He can do anything he wants, all by himself. Joshua saw God drop food from the sky for forty years to feed the children of Israel. He saw the Lord produce water from a rock. These were independent acts of God.

But when it came time to fight this battle, Joshua realized that God takes pleasure when his children participate in his purposes. He had confidence that the Lord would defeat his enemies. But God wouldn't magically whisk the Israelites to the winner's circle. They'd have to march all night. Use their swords. Devise plans. Bleed. Kill. Risk. *Act.*

Audacious faith is not passive. Neither is audacious prayer. Every aspiration you have in prayer needs an accompanying action. Otherwise, you're not really praying. You're just pontificating.

You do the natural. Trust God for the super.

Now you're praying Sun Stand Still prayers. Now this is moving beyond fantasyland. Now you're walking in real audacious faith.

A Tale of Two Dreamers

There's a big difference between standing in hope and walking in faith. Let me explain it from the perspective of two men with an identical dream—and radically different results.

* ✳ My friend Jack is an extremely talented musician. But I don't think you'll ever hear any of his songs. In fact, I'm sure you won't. And it's not because they're not

good. Jack has recorded some great stuff over the last fifteen years. But it's rotting on the hard drive of his computer in his home studio.

There was a time when Jack envisioned having a ministry to Christians all over the world through his songs. He prayed a lot about it. Talked a lot about it. Worked really hard on it. Invested a lot of time and money in it. The people around him sacrificed a lot for it too. His wife earned a living to support him and the kids so that he could stay home and chase his dream. And after fifteen years of writing music, making plans, and fearing failure, Jack has still never released a single album publicly. He doesn't perform any concerts anywhere. And he recently decided to stop writing music.

The last time I talked to Jack, he seemed worn down and embarrassed about his lack of progress. I told him he shouldn't be so hard on himself. He said yes, he should. He clarified that he wasn't so much embarrassed about his lack of progress as he was about his lack of faith. He never had the courage to put his music out there and trust God with the results. Now, he said, he's too old to tour, to break through, or to care. He just wants to pay his mortgage, and he's come to terms with the fact that the world will never hear his music. He doesn't even go to church anymore. I think he's embarrassed to show his face, because he feels like he's let down all the people who have prayed for his music career. He feels like a loser. He oozes with regret.

✳ My friend Matt is also a gifted Christian singer/song-writer. Lots of people have heard his music. You may even have sung one of his songs in your church last weekend. Now, I don't think that Matt is more talented than Jack. But he has actually taken action to get the music that was in him *out there.* He started his career by singing his songs for almost any group that would listen. Sometimes that meant playing for six teenagers in a moldy lodge at a youth ministry ski retreat. Other times that meant slipping his songs between Skynyrd covers at a bar. But he played a lot. Every chance he got. And he always had faith that God would allow him to touch the world through his music. He's believed that as long as I've known him. And he's taken consistent actions that give feet to that belief.

So God has given him a lot of success. Matt's platform has steadily increased over the last fifteen years. At one point, a lot of people told Matt he was going over the edge when he relocated his family to another part of the country to be closer to the epicenter of the Christian music industry. But Matt wanted to go over the edge. He dared to believe God for the impossible.

He stays on the road most of the year, playing his music—now for much larger crowds. When he's home, he leads worship in his church for thousands of people, and he writes music that usually gets recorded by other well-known artists. His Sun Stand Still prayer is that God will allow him to influence the body of Christ all over the world to dream big and glorify Jesus through worship.

STOP STANDING IN HOPE

Too many Christians end up like Jack. I want you to end up like Matt. I know there's good music inside you. There are concepts and contributions flowing inside you that need to be released for the world to hear.

But a Page 23 vision isn't any good to anyone if it doesn't make it out of the home studio. Audacious faith is the backbeat that gives your God-inspired intentions a groove worth moving to.

Praying Sun Stand Still prayers isn't about thinking audacious thoughts. It's about activating audacious faith. It's about making your move. Pushing while you pray. I like the old King James Version's translation of Hebrews 11:1:

> Faith is the *substance* of things hoped for, the *evidence* of things not seen.

Faith is not an abstract theoretical proposition. It's not wishful thinking. It's substance. It's action.

Most of my life I imagined faith as some kind of force field. And the way we talk about faith dematerializes it. By most definitions, faith is synonymous with hope. But the more I study Scripture, the more I detect a sharp distinction between hope and faith.

My friend Jack *hoped* to inspire thousands of people through his music. But he never merged his hope with the faith to make it happen. Now his hope is running out because his *faith* never kicked in.

The scary thing about Jack is that the thing he was hoping for was right on the money. He didn't do anything bad or wrong to sabotage his destiny. He just didn't activate his vision by applying and exerting his faith. He let his fear get the better of him.

Matt activated his hope by walking in faith rather than just standing in hope. Because of that, he's seeing his Page 23 vision come to life in more fresh and remarkable ways than he ever imagined. People all over the planet sing songs that he wrote in his living room—because he activated his dream by faith.

Hope is a *desire*. Faith is a *demonstration*. Hope *wants* it to happen. Faith *causes* it to happen and acts as if it's already done.

Faith is not content to want it really, *really* bad. Faith consults the drawings and gets busy building. Hope is the blueprint. Faith is the contractor.

Some of the impossible things we're believing God for will never happen in our lives if we *stand in hope instead of walking in faith*.

Both Jack and Matt had a dream planted inside their hearts. The same dream. But only one of them brought that dream full term and gave birth—because only one of them pushed.

It's truly amazing that God answers our Sun Stand Still prayers in ways that only he can. But it's equally amazing that we get to play a part in God's fulfilling his promise. Joshua was part of the miracle that was God's answer. Joshua was part of the answer to his own prayer.

If you're going to believe audaciously, be prepared to act audaciously. Part of the answer to your Sun Stand Still prayer just might be you.

CHAPTER 18

From the Promise
to the Payoff

Here's the irony about having an audacious vision: Sometimes you have to close your eyes in order to see it. It's easy to keep believing in your vision once you start getting visible results. When God starts fulfilling his promises in tangible ways, your faith gains momentum. When the answer to your prayers is already in progress, your audacity begins to build on itself. But while you're waiting for things to get moving, it can be grueling. The time between the conception and the completion of a vision will test the limits of your faith. And a lot of people fail the test. In fact, most people give up on their Page 23 vision way too soon—before they ever get to see their Sun Stand Still prayer answered.

Hopefully by now the pieces of your Page 23 vision are beginning to come together. You may not have all the details. Honestly, nobody does. But I hope you're getting a stronger sense of something bigger that God wants to do through your life. And the more your excitement builds inside about that vision, the more you're going to want it to take shape immediately. Nobody can relate to that sensation more than I can.

Personally, I'm addicted to progress. And I have a short supply of patience. If God gives me a vision for my ministry, my family, my health, or my finances today, I want to see it accomplished quickly. Say, like yesterday. I get super frustrated with any lag time between hearing God's voice and seeing the finished product. I want to experience the accomplishment of the vision without having to sit in the waiting room.

Vision doesn't work on that timetable. If it did, you wouldn't need faith. If all your prayers were answered the moment you prayed them, you'd start putting your faith in the power of your prayers instead of the power of Jesus.

I realize it sounds like I'm contradicting myself here. I've told you to expect God to make the sun stand still. I've tried to convince you that God is able to set the ordinary activities in your life ablaze with his glory. And ultimately, that God wants to do so much through you at such a rate and on such a scale that the watching world will know it could *only* be him.

I mean every word of it. That's the story of my life. God has given me opportunities that defy my age and lack of experience. So I certainly don't want to undermine your faith to believe that he can do the same kinds of things for you. He can—and will—deliver on every promise he ever makes to you. In other words, when God makes a promise, there's always a payoff.

Just ask Joshua. God told him that he would have success everywhere he went.

Phenomenal promise.

Joshua went on to lead Israel to occupy the land that had

been out of their reach since the time God had promised it to Abraham.

Payoff.

But how about all the stuff in the middle? How about all the lives that were lost under Joshua's command to achieve the ultimate victories? How about the embarrassing defeat at Ai, where Joshua's side was routed by an army that was clearly inferior? How about all the grueling desert marches and the thousands of hours of exhausting strategic planning? We've got to account for all the uncertainty, anxiety, change, and sacrifice that came with the package. The story behind the glory.

That's called the *process*.

Between the promise and the payoff there's always a process. That process is where your audacious faith comes into play. Without the process, there is no progress. But the process is usually filled with pain. And if you don't know how to process the process, you probably won't make it to your promised land.

That's why audacious faith is so vital. It brings your unseen future possibilities into focus right now. It redirects your attention from what *is* right now to what you believe *will be* one day. And it ensures that you don't give up in the meantime—before you ever get to see your dream become a reality.

WHEN THERE'S NOTHING TO SEE

Every big dream has a small beginning. No exceptions. Every tree was a seed once upon a time. The people who do big things for God are the ones who have the perspective to see the potential in these small beginnings. They refuse to stop nurturing the seed until the dream is full grown. They have the tenacity to stay after it, even if it isn't lucrative, exciting, or remarkable in its current form. Through the power of audacious faith, they get a Page 23 vision from God, saturate it in Sun Stand Still prayer, and embrace the process—until the payoff is in plain view.

That's not as easy as it sounds. Suppose your Sun Stand Still prayer is, *God, I want all my children to grow up to love Jesus and impact their generation.* If your fourteen-year-old daughter is screaming at her eleven-year-old brother in the background while you're praying that prayer, it can be hard to keep your eyes on the prize.

Or let's say you've never been in good physical shape in your adult life, and your Sun Stand Still prayer is, *Lord, enable me with the discipline to lose eighty-five pounds this year and keep it off.* If you're so sore after your first comeback trip to the gym that you can barely walk to the refrigerator to get your Slim-Fast shake, it's tough to want to go back for round two.

How do you keep moving forward when you're not sure you're really getting anywhere? How do you keep your vision in sight when there's nothing to see?

We've already spent a little time getting acquainted with Elijah, one of my favorite Old Testament juggernauts. He had guts. He risked his life by getting in King Ahab's face and telling him that, because of the nation's wickedness, there would be no rain in the land for three years. Guess what? It didn't rain for three years. Eventually the rain returned, proving to all of Israel that the Lord God was indeed the only true God, and they needed to turn back to him. In this process God wiped out all the false prophets on a mountain called Carmel. It's a thrilling and well-known story recorded in 1 Kings 18.

I've heard a lot of sermons about the showdown on Mount Carmel. How God sent fire from heaven, and how Elijah destroyed all the false prophets. And I guess I assumed that, immediately after the showdown, the rain came pouring down. In my imagination, the moment the nation repented and professed their allegiance to God, there was a big thunderclap and the bottom fell out of the sky—on the spot.

Turns out that it didn't happen that way. There's a bonus scene at the end of chapter 18. It's not nearly as well known, but it's essential to the story—and full of insight.

After putting all the false prophets to death, Elijah assured King Ahab of "the sound of a heavy rain" (verse 41). He wanted the king to be certain that a storm was in the immediate forecast. But next, Elijah did something rather strange. While Ahab went back down the mountain to eat and drink, Elijah went in the other direction, back toward the top of Mount Carmel. And when he got to the summit, he bent down and put his head between his knees. Right away, he sent his servant to go and look toward the sea, presumably to check on whether the rain was rolling in yet.

And the servant came back with what had to be the worst possible report: "There is nothing there" (verse 43).

That's the last thing Elijah wanted to hear. Everything was on the line here—his own credibility and, more importantly, the reputation of his God. He had just promised the king in front of the whole nation that the three-year drought was over. And he wasn't speaking on his own authority. God himself had commanded Elijah to appear to Ahab and bring the dry spell to a close. Not only that, but Elijah had heard the sound with his own ears. He felt the rumbling. But when his servant scanned the sky, things didn't look so good. Not a single sign of precipitation in the sky.

There is nothing there.

I think this is the perfect analogy to describe the formation of audacious dreams. Vision begins when you hear the sound of God's voice speaking something to your heart. It's not an audible voice. It's more like an unshakable impression, an inner sense. You hear God telling you to step out and start your own company. You hear God challenging you to go back to school and finish your degree. You hear God calling you to keep yourself sexually pure.

So you commit to God's vision, go to the top of your Mount Carmel, and look to the sea for the payoff. But often, at that point, you see absolutely nothing. And most of the time, no one around you sees anything either.

There is nothing there. No confirmation. No turnaround. No breakthrough.

This is enough to make most people doubt their dream. But I want you to notice something about Elijah that you may have overlooked. He never actually looked for the clouds. He didn't look at anything, actually. He was bowed to the ground with his face between his knees. I don't think this was coincidental. I think it was a strategic move on Elijah's part. And it illustrates a fundamental principle of audacious faith: when what you see around you doesn't match up with what God has spoken inside you, you've got to hold on to what you've heard. Paul said it more plainly in 2 Corinthians 5:7:

We live by faith, not by sight.

Elijah didn't waver in his faith because of limited visibility. He held on to the things he had heard. He had heard God's instruction to prophesy the end of the drought. He had heard the sound of heavy rain. And he refused to second-guess God's purpose in this situation. Instead of giving up, he sent his servant back to look again. And again. And again. Six times the servant went back to look for clouds. Six times there was nothing there. That had to get old for this poor fellow. And surely by now Elijah was beginning to wonder.

But suddenly, the seventh time, a little bit of hope stuck out in the sky. Just a little bit. The servant reported it to Elijah this way: "A cloud as small as a man's hand is rising from the sea" (verse 44).

Just a small cloud. But that was enough proof for Elijah. He commanded his servant, "Go and tell Ahab, 'Hitch up your chariot and go down before the rain stops you' " (verse 44). And not long after that, the windows of heaven opened and the rain came pouring down. The agony of a three-year drought came to an end. Elijah was vindicated. A whole nation witnessed the strength and provision of God at a new level.

But it didn't happen all at once. Before there was a downpour—before there was even a drizzle, for that matter—there were three long years of parched ground, crop failure, and famine. And there was the faith of one man who held on to what he had heard, even when he couldn't see any signs in the sky.

A Cloud the Size of This Boy's Hand

The ability to stay tuned in to what you've heard when you can't see any proof is what separates audacious faith from wishful thinking. The rain doesn't fall the first time you look for it. You have to keep going back again and again and again. And you've got to make a big deal out of your small beginnings.

Maybe you have a family member who is far from God. Your

Sun Stand Still prayer is that God would change her heart and raise her up to be a leader. Naturally, you want to see a lot of change in a little bit of time. But don't expect your sister to become a Christian, memorize the book of Ephesians, write three Christian songs, and adopt an orphan from Haiti by next Tuesday. Anticipate a small start. Celebrate when you see a little cloud in the sky. And make preparation for the heavy rain that's sure to follow.

One of my biggest Sun Stand Still prayers after I gave my life to Christ as a high-school junior was that my dad would get into a right relationship with God. My dad is a good man and always did his best to be a good dad. He coached my baseball teams. He showed up for my wrestling tournaments. He told me he loved me, and he taught me all the basics. He even taught me how to throw the first punch in a fight, remember?

But my dad has also had a pretty rough life. And he's beat some tremendous odds. When my father was nine years old, his dad killed himself. It actually happened on my dad's ninth birthday. That was his birthday present: finding out his own father had ended his life. I've always thought that was about the saddest thing a boy could experience. But I think this is even sadder: his dad was such a violent and abusive drunk that it was a relief to see him go.

Because he grew up in a poor family without a father, my dad had to drop out of school in the eighth grade to start working. In that sense, growing up fatherless caused him to develop a strong work ethic. But it also gave him room to experiment heavily with drugs and alcohol.

Those experiments eventually turned into addictions, and early on in life, my dad was a certified alcoholic. He got married and divorced twice before he met my mom. And when they got married and had me, my mom was able to get him clean and straighten him up—for a little while.

Soon, after a nasty job loss that left him bitter and skeptical, he turned back to drinking and his favorite drug, marijuana. Those addictions had a lot of control over his life for many years. But since he was a highly functional alcoholic, he held down several jobs at a time, did his part with the family, and came across as a pretty normal guy. But he told me later that when he would wake up every morning with his head still pounding from drinking until midnight the night before, knowing he was setting a terrible example for his kids, he would beg God to somehow rescue him from it all.

By the time I got serious about my faith, my dad was completely MIA, spiritually speaking. Since my mom was the glue that held the family together, she'd make sure we got up every Sunday and made it to church on time. She'd always done that—without fail. My dad would cook breakfast for the family, then head off to the par-three golf course with his buddies to get drunk while his wife and kids went to church.

I was a few months into my relationship with Jesus, and I was on fire. Since I had already been praying for all my pot-smoking friends to get right with God, naturally I started praying really hard for my pot-smoking dad. But one day, just praying for him didn't seem sufficient. I decided to step out and say something to him.

I'm not quite sure what came over me. I didn't know it at the time, but it turned out to be my first major taste of audacious faith. It was a typical Sunday morning. Dad was cleaning up the dishes from breakfast. The rest of the family was getting dressed for church. And I asked my dad to stop what he was doing, because I had something important to tell him.

"Dad, God is about to get hold of your life. I don't know exactly how or when, but I think it's going to be soon. And when he does, everything is going to change. I just wanted to tell you that."

I wasn't trying to preach at him. I sincerely believed I had heard from God the same words I said to him. I wasn't rude or disrespectful. I think it came across as heartfelt and genuine.

He didn't say much in response. He did nod. But then he finished washing the dishes. And we went to church while he went to the golf course to drink.

Nothing changed right away. My mom continued to pray fervently for my dad every day, just like she had for the past twenty years. I tried to be the best example of a Christian that I could the rest of the time I lived under their roof. Months passed. A year later, I went off to a college that was a four-hour drive away from home. But I stayed connected with my parents. And in the middle of my freshman year of college, I noticed from a distance that something was starting to shift in my dad's life.

He stopped drinking. Not for a few weeks. For several months. He told me all about it when he came to hear me preach at a local church, where I was serving with my college ministry team. And it seemed like he was coming to hear me preach a lot. Now, it didn't surprise me that he was coming to support his boy. But sometimes he would drive a hundred miles just to hear me preach a fifteen-minute sermon. It was a small start. A cloud the size of a boy's hand. But God was up to something big.

Just before my sophomore year started, I was scheduled to preach at my home church in Moncks Corner. Of course, Mom and Dad were there. And at the end of my sermon (which couldn't have been very good, because I had no idea how to preach), I gave an invitation for people to come to the altar and give their lives to Jesus. Then I turned it over to my pastor and sat down in the front row, closed my eyes, and prayed for all the people coming forward.

I was a little annoyed when I felt someone sit beside me and tap me on the shoulder. It seemed inappropriate for anyone to interrupt the preacher's prayer time. When I looked up, my pastor was sitting beside me, and I could tell he was excited.

"Steven," he said, "you may want to take a look down there at the altar."

And when I scanned the front of that little Baptist church, I saw the answer to the hundreds of prayers my mom had prayed. And the audacious statement I made in the kitchen two years earlier came full circle. My dad was kneeling at the altar, crying like a baby, dedicating his life to Christ.

I hurried to the front to kneel and pray with him. It was an incredible moment. But it was infinitely more than a moment. It was the beginning of a complete revolution in my dad's life that continues to this day. He hasn't had a drop of alcohol to drink in more than ten years. He's survived cancer. He's been a Sunday-school teacher, founded a ministry for homeless men, and memorized the entire Sermon on the Mount as well as the book of James. Not bad for an eighth-grade dropout.

I was having a conversation with my dad recently about our little conversation in the kitchen so many years before. He confessed to me, "Boy, when you told me God was going to change my life, I actually felt sorry for you. I thought, *I hope this poor kid doesn't get his hopes up. He has no idea how bad off I actually am.* But you had faith. Thank you for believing."

Small Beginning to Big Finish

The situation around you may look nothing like the vision God has put inside you. But by the power of faith, you can turn your small beginning into a grand finale. Here's the way Jesus put it in Matthew 17:20:

> I tell you the truth, if you have faith as small as a mustard
> seed, you can say to this mountain, "Move from here to
> there" and it will move. Nothing will be impossible for you.

The tiniest seed of faith, applied and exerted consistently over the course of time, can move the biggest mountain in your life. Having the faith to start small in the face of the most overwhelming odds is about as audacious as it gets.

If your Sun Stand Still prayer is to be completely debt free so that you can live an extremely generous life, start small. Don't let the remaining balances overshadow your gradual progress. As you take baby steps of faith, celebrate each milestone along the way. Build on the success of paying off your first credit card. Use the momentum to pay down another. Then another. Then another. You may be able to give only a meager percentage back to God at first. But start there. And increase your giving by 2 or 5 or 10 percent every year. Eventually you'll be shocked at the audacious amounts of money you're able to give away to support God's work in the world.

Holly and I made two financial promises to each other when we got married. We committed to always put God first by giving at least 10 percent of all our income back to him. And we committed to staying completely free of consumer debt. We wanted to get in a position to write our largest check each month to the local church, not the mortgage company. We've been blown away by God's faithfulness to increase our capacity to give year after year for the last eight years. When we started giving 10 percent of our income away, it didn't seem like much. But every year, we've raised that percentage a little bit. And when we were looking at our records at the end of last year, we honestly couldn't believe how much money we had been able to give to our church. The amount we gave away in that one year far exceeded our total household income in the first year of our marriage—just eight years earlier.

God has blessed us with more than enough, not only to meet our needs, but also to meet the needs of people all around the world through strategic giving. It didn't get that way overnight. We took small steps toward our big dream of radical generosity. And God has fulfilled his promise to make his resources overflow in our lives. The payoff is the satisfaction and peace in knowing that the kingdom of God is our greatest investment. And it has been possible only because we took the baby steps of audacious faith.

This may seem like a small, isolated example to you. But that's the point. I'm trying to get you to see that you need to work what you've got and build on small successes if you're going to ever fully realize your God-sized vision.

And of course, this doesn't apply just to finances. Do you have a strained relationship with your teenage son? Is your Sun Stand

Still prayer that God would restore that relationship and bring your family into harmony? Start small. Work what you've got. Before you go to sleep tonight, find one positive thing you can verbally affirm in the life of your child. Swallow your pride. Push your fears aside. And speak something positive to your son. I doubt he'll respond right away by hugging you and filling you in on the darkest secrets of his life, asking for your wisdom and guidance, heeding your every instruction, and offering to mow the lawn every Tuesday. But a seed has been planted. And whether you see it or not, God will start to water that seed. If you continue to plant, over time, there may come a day when you see signs of life springing up all around you. But it doesn't start with a harvest. It starts with a seed that initiates a process.

The Process Is the Point

Too many people forget the promise and forfeit the payoff because they faint in the process. It's human nature to want to skip straight from the promise to the payoff. Who doesn't want to get right to the good stuff? But the process is invaluable. The process is a time of strengthening. The process is the place where you lay down your pride and learn to rely totally on God. Most importantly, the process is the way we grow to know God. And that's really the whole point.

One of my major pet peeves is when someone spoils the plot of a movie I was planning to see. Because when they tell me that the dude dies at the end, or that the boy gets the girl, or that the team wins the championship, or whatever, it ruins the experience. See, if I wanted to know just the outcome, I would have read the plot summary on Wikipedia. But that's not the goal when you see a movie. You want to feel tension and suspense. You want to wonder whether the good guy wins or the relationship works out. The plot is the point.

What if the same dynamic that makes the plot the point of a movie applies to our relationship with God? Is it possible that the process isn't just a time waster or a commercial break? Have you ever considered that, in the overall scheme of God's design, the process is the point?

If all God wanted to do was get right to the happy ending, you'd be in heaven by now. If his only intention were to make your dreams come true, he'd snap his fingers and your vision would appear out of thin air. But that's not all God wants. And deep down, it's not really all you want either. You want to learn to walk by faith, not by sight. And you can't learn that without walking through periods of complete darkness. The apprehension and gut-level fear you'll feel in these stages may make you turn back and pursue something safer.

Or you can opt for something better. You can embrace the process with audacious faith. Because every big dream has small beginnings. Between the promise and the payoff, there's always a process.

And that process is the breeding ground of faith. That process has the potential to draw you closer to Jesus than you've ever been before.

The process is the point.

CHAPTER 19

Ten Guidelines for a Sun Stand Still Prayer

You have no idea how much it goes against the grain of my personality to write ten dimensions or five truths or steps to anything. In my experience, not much in life happens according to a defined numerical order or other rigid process. Especially when it comes to prayer.

But on the other hand, there's nothing closer to my heart than my desire for audacious faith to be more than a concept you read about in a book—and then forget. I want to bury it in your soul. I want to make it a permanent part of your character. I want to shoot it like an arrow into your future.

And so, to help you remember and apply what I've been teaching, I ask you to take hold of the following truths and steps as your personal action plan to live and pray audaciously for God.

Burn them into your imagination and memory—and put them to work in your life.

FIVE TRUTHS ABOUT
SUN STAND STILL PRAYERS

Truth 1: *A Sun Stand Still Prayer Is Audacious*

To be audacious, a Sun Stand Still prayer addresses a need or a goal that is far beyond your ability to meet it. You know it will never happen unless God intervenes. But it also shouldn't be outside the realm of your personal faith capacity. The Bible talks about different measures of faith—that each of us should use what we have. And so a Sun Stand Still prayer should be so big that you could never *achieve* it on your own, but it shouldn't be bigger than your ability to *believe* that God can achieve it.

You may not be ready to pray that God could make your family computer business the next Apple. But you could conceivably pray that God would enable you to operate with total integrity, give 10 percent of your revenue to alleviate poverty, and have one of the lowest turnover rates in the industry. Or something like that. Start there.

Truth 2: *A Sun Stand Still Prayer Is Specific*

Make your Sun Stand Still specific: in fact, the more specific it is, the better. *I want to bring God glory through my life* isn't nearly as good as, *By the time I leave this job, I want to earn the right to have a conversation within my department about my faith in Jesus Christ.* If your Sun Stand Still prayer is too vague, you won't know what corresponding actions to take to bring your faith to life.

Write it down. Commit to it. Put it in a place that will remind you to pray and inspire you to act. And when God answers, write that down too—it will become a memorial that will inspire you to pray audaciously as a way of life.

Truth 3: A Sun Stand Still Prayer Doesn't Have to Be Permanent

Your Sun Stand Still prayer doesn't have to last forever. I've prayed Sun Stand Still prayers that were accomplished in three weeks. I thanked God and moved on to a new Sun Stand Still prayer. On the other hand, I've got some Sun Stand Still prayers that have been in process for years. I'm still standing in faith and trusting God's timing on those.

Truth 4: A Sun Stand Still Prayer May Be Too Personal to Share with Others

Personal Sun Stand Still prayers are often the most important ones. Some of the sin issues you're dealing with may be embarrassing, or some needs you face may be demoralizing. When you find an area of your life in which the need is so personal that you don't even know how to talk about it, you've found a good foundation to build a Sun Stand Still prayer on.

Truth 5: A Sun Stand Still Prayer Thrives with a Team

Faith is contagious. You will be empowered when you surround yourself with people who will help to bear the burden of your Sun Stand Still prayer. They'll help you keep the vision in sight when there's nothing to see. They'll remind you of God's faithfulness when your own faith is faltering. They'll increase the effectiveness of your prayer exponentially by joining their faith with yours.

I don't know exactly where you'll find this kind of community. It will probably look different depending on your stage of life. Most Christians find their faith team through the local church. Not just the Sunday morning gathering, either, but also small groups where you can dig deeper. The important thing isn't necessarily *where* you find this support but *that you do find it.* No one's faith can survive for long alone.

Based on those five truths, let's explore the practical steps to making prayers of audacious faith an everyday part of your life.

FIVE STEPS TO A SUN STAND STILL PRAYER

Step 1: Activate Your Audacious Faith

Reject passivity and fear. Seize the initiative because you know who God is. He is good, and he is strong. Agree with God that he has called you to a larger purpose for your life that will bring him glory. This is your Page 23 vision, and it's always a purpose that only he can accomplish.

> Have I not commanded you? Be strong and courageous. Do not be terrified; do not be discouraged, for the LORD your God will be with you wherever you go. (Joshua 1:9)

Step 2: Approach God with Boldness

Come before God with confidence, making your request to him (we called it building a case) based on his proven character, the promises in his Word, and his actions in the past. This does not mean his answers are in any way connected to your worthiness. Rather, pray humbly, based on grace, because you *don't* want what you deserve.

This is the confidence we have in approaching God: that if we ask anything according to his will, he hears us. And if we know that he hears us—whatever we ask—we know that we have what we asked of him. (1 John 5:14–15)

Step 3: Ask specifically for What Is Humanly Impossible

Like Joshua, speak your exact request to God without mumbling or hesitation, believing that *nothing* is impossible with him. Because if we have the audacity to ask, God has the ability to perform. And you have now chosen to see your situation from God's point of view, not yours. You're asking for something that only he can accomplish—and that only he can take credit for.

For nothing is impossible with God. (Luke 1:37)

Everything is possible for him who believes. (Mark 9:23)

Step 4: Advance Toward the Answer

To advance toward the answer, you must "push while you pray." Joshua didn't just pray for a victory in battle. He marched all night so that he would be in a position to defeat the enemy when God answered his prayer. Jonathan didn't just believe that God might give him the victory at the top of the cliff; he started climbing the cliff. Audacious faith means that you are willing to become the answer to your own prayer. Make your move. Be prepared to work hard, and stick with it.

Faith by itself, if it is not accompanied by action, is dead. (James 2:17)

Step 5: Give God All the Glory

When God does the impossible, give him all the glory—the credit, honor, and thanks he deserves. As we say often at Elevation Church, what God has done among us is so big that there's nobody to blame but him. The stories of our Sun Stand Still prayers are ours to tell—but *the story itself is always all about Jesus.*

> O LORD, you are my God;
>   I will exalt you and your name,
> for in perfect faithfulness
>   you have done marvelous things. (Isaiah 25:1)

CHAPTER 20

In the Middle
of a Move of God

Years ago, I was wrapping up a meeting with a good Christian man, and he asked if he could pray for me. Usually I'd accept that offer without hesitation. After all, "Can I pray for you?" is a pretty standard request between Christians. But coming from this guy, I wasn't so sure. I had to think about it for a minute.

This brother wasn't an average believer. He was a modern-day Joshua, the leader of one of the largest underground church movements in China—or in the world, for that matter. He was responsible for the oversight of *1.8 million people* through his house church movement.

He was only fifty-one years old but looked eighty because of the hell he'd been through. He'd been imprisoned five times for a total of three years. He'd been tortured for Christ on many occasions. Of course, he refuses to talk about it, because he is too focused on the gospel to talk about himself. But I'd heard the stories.

This man had endured things for the sake of Jesus that made

my everyday prayers for safety, comfort, and blessing seem trivial—and a little embarrassing. And since he wasn't an average believer, I realized he was probably not going to pray an average prayer for me.

So, did I really want him to pray for me? That depended on what he was going to pray for. Was I ready to accept the consequences? If he were to ask God to lead me through hard places, would I want to follow? If he were to ask the Lord to perform the kinds of miracles in my life that would seem strange to everyone else around me, would I be okay with that?

I was nervous, but I agreed, bowed my head, and let the man pray. He laid his hands on me and wept for over ten minutes as he asked God to bless me. I didn't understand a word he was saying. He didn't speak English, I didn't speak Mandarin, and it just didn't feel appropriate to have a translator get up in the middle of such a holy moment.

When he finished, he hugged me and told me through the interpreter that he wanted to take a picture of me so he could put it in his Bible and keep praying for me. I told the interpreter I would be honored...under one condition. He had to give me a summary of the prayer that my new friend and hero in the faith had just prayed.

So the interpreter gave me the highlights in broken English: "He prayed that God would give you wisdom and that your faith would be a model that would spread to other Christians and churches all over the world."

I'm glad I let the man of God pray for me.

And now I want to pray for you. Not that I'm a giant in the faith compared to this man who has laid his life down for the cause of Christ again and again. But still, I want to pray for you.

Because I want this book to become so much more than another source of *information* for your already overcrowded spiritual file. You've learned how to develop a Page 23 vision. You're aware of the cost of your calling. You've seen a basic profile of the goodness and greatness of God to frame up the potential of your life. This is all crucial information. Stuff you've got to know if you're going to believe God for the impossible. But information alone isn't the wellspring of audacious faith.

I don't even want this message to stop at the point of *inspiration,* although I pray you're incredibly inspired by the message you've just experienced. You should be. Your ordinary life is about to be ignited for God's glory. Your uniqueness is going to be leveraged for Kingdom purposes. Your small beginnings will have seismic impact. And even your most challenging crisis or painful failure is an opportunity for God's glory to shine in your life. But inspiration alone won't propel you through the process of activating your faith.

What you need is an *impartation,* if you'll permit me to use a good old preacher word. You need the words that you've heard and the concepts you've understood to be transferred wholly from me to you…to become a catalyst in your life that gets down deeper than logic and grips you more tightly than emotion…and changes your life through the power of God's Spirit.

I think you're ready to believe God for the impossible. You're ready to pray a Sun Stand Still prayer that will be the stepping-stone to participating in the impossible. And you won't be praying alone. *Sun Stand Still* isn't just an individual message. This has the potential to launch a movement of believers all over the planet.

When you begin to activate your faith and pray Sun Stand

Still prayers, you're doing more than just changing *your* life. You're placing yourself in the middle of a move of God.

You're participating in a mission to manifest the kingdom of God in every sphere of your influence. *You're responding to God's call to Christians everywhere to embrace, harness, and ultimately shape the culture.* And together, we are a powerful force.

Our message—the message of forgiveness and grace in Jesus Christ—is the most relevant message in the history of the world. We can't *be timid about it.*

We believe that since our God is the Author of all things compassionate and creative, the church of Jesus Christ should be the most compassionate and creative entity on the planet.

We know what we believe, we know why we believe it, and we're determined to live it out with all our hearts. We're not *perfect,* but our passion is sincere to the bone. We're not here to merely *survive* or to *condemn* the world, but to transform it for the glory of God. And we're *here to stay.*

We're the living, breathing, forcefully advancing people of God. We are a generation of Joshuas.

See, I'm not praying just that God would give you the boldness to pray that the sun would stand still. I'm praying that the sun would stand still over an entire *generation* of Christians, transforming everything we touch. God promised to give Joshua and the Israelites every place where they set their feet. Are we ready to take that kind of ground for the kingdom of God?

I'm sure you're asking yourself the same question I asked that day the leader of the underground church movement laid his hands on me: *Am I really ready for this prayer? Am I really ready to take my place in the middle of a move of God?*

I believe you are. I believe God has been preparing you for this all your life. And this is my prayer for you.

For your family...

I'm praying that the sun will stand still over your family. If there are broken relationships between you and your parents, brothers, or sisters, I pray that God will heal them. If you're in a place of isolation and loneliness, I pray that God will draw near to you and give you comfort. If your children have drifted from the center of God's love, I pray that God will draw them back. If your spouse has shut down emotionally, I pray that God will open her heart.

If you are a student...

I'm praying that the sun will stand still over your school. That you will never be ashamed of the gospel of Jesus. That you will choose a higher standard. Refuse to sacrifice eternal reward on the altar of temporary pleasure. Pray unlikely prayers. Risk your popularity for the sake of a greater glory. Identify with your Savior. Lay a foundation for a life of destiny.

For your job...

I'm praying that the sun will stand still over the company where you go to work every day. I don't care whether you sweep the floors or run the company—I'm asking God to illuminate your purpose and show you off like a trophy. I pray that many will come to know Christ through your example and that you will make the mark on the world that only you can make. After all, God doesn't call his people to live in the confines of the ghetto of subcultural Christianity. We are image bearers of God, determined to represent Christ in all fields: educational, medical, legal, industrial, financial... May you proclaim Christ in all things.

For you as a child of God, deeply loved by him...

I'm praying that the sun will stand still over all your hopes and dreams and the issues of your heart. That you will confess every past mistake to God and let him redeem it. That you will bring every unfulfilled expectation to God and let him exceed it. That you will expose every sinful area in your life to God and let him transform it. That you will offer all your talents, gifts, and skills to God and let him use them.

The world is waiting for change. God's people are the change the world is waiting for. So seize the vision. Activate audacious faith. Make your move.

This is how it feels to share the stage with Joshua.

This is how it feels to believe God for the impossible.

This is how it feels to see the sun stand still.

Welcome to the middle of a move of God.

Acknowledgments

Holly: You didn't help me do it. You made me do it.
   I love you.
Elijah and Graham: Technically, you weren't much help.
   But you're my best friends and the greatest men of
   God of your generation.
Faith and L-Train: You don't have to hope it's a good life.
   It *is* a good life.
Murrill and Deborah: Thanks for the wife. You did good.
   I love your family.
Chunks and Amy C.: You said yes. We've come a long
   way. Worth the trip.
Core Team: I told you so. You're the reason.
Staff: This is that. We are the generation.
Craig G.: Thanks for taking me further, faster. I'll do my
   best to make you proud.
Clayton K., Perry N., Terrell M., Ron C., Ed Y., Mark B.:
   My big brothers and lifesavers. I honor you.
Tom W.: You're no joke.
David K.: We got the stallions in the barn. Thanks for
   pushing me and for teaching me that every line
   doesn't have to be retweetable and I don't have to talk
   so loud (all the time).
The team at WaterBrook Multnomah: I prayed for someone to believe in this message and take a chance on
   me. Thank you. Really.

Acknowledgments

Joyebatka: Warriors...

Paul C. and Eric S.: You worked hard. You made it better.

Eric and Nicole P.: The best friends ever.

The Elevation Nation: The best is ahead.

About the Author

Steven Furtick grew up in the small town of Moncks Corner, South Carolina, where at age sixteen he felt clearly called by God to start a life-changing church in a major city in the future.

This vision became a reality when Steven and seven other families risked everything—sold houses, quit jobs, and moved to Charlotte, North Carolina—to plant a new church, believing that God would turn the city upside down for his glory. That risk birthed Elevation Church and has resulted in a remarkable return. Through God's favor and a relentless pursuit of their mission to see *people far from God filled with life in Christ,* in just four years Elevation has seen thousands of professions of faith and grown to more than six thousand in weekly attendance. Because of this explosive growth, Elevation Church was named one of the ten fastest growing churches in America by *Outreach Magazine* in 2007, 2008, and 2009.

The heart of Steven's message is revolutionary faith and how to approach every experience from a visionary perspective. His passion for seeing God's purposes fulfilled in our day is igniting a fire in the city of Charlotte and throughout the United States.

Steven holds a degree in communication from North Greenville University and a master of divinity degree from Southern Baptist Theological Seminary. He lives in the Charlotte area with his wife, Holly, and their two sons, Elijah and Graham.

You can follow Steven and access hundreds of resources to activate your faith at www.stevenfurtick.com.

SUN STAND STILL

THE MOVEMENT

WHAT'S AVAILABLE ONLINE:

Share your own Sun Stand Still prayer at
www.sunstandstill.org and attend a live
Prayer Experience

Group discussion short films
led by Steven Furtick

Study materials for students, groups,
churches or ministries

Free church resources and media to participate
in the Sun Stand Still series

WWW.SUNSTANDSTILL.ORG